FAST MONEY, EASY MONEY

Unlock the Secrets of Wealth with a Proven, Step-by-Step System

written by

Braxton R. Meeks

*To everyone daring
to dream bigger, act faster,
and build wealth that lasts a lifetime.*

FAST MONEY, EASY MONEY:

Unlock the Secrets of Wealth with a Proven, Step-by-Step System

Written By
Braxton R. Meeks

Images & Fullcover By
Sun Child Wind Spirit

Proofread By
Joaquin Mann

Edited By
Mylia Tiye Mal Jaza

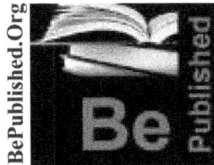

BePublished.Org

Be Published

First Edition. Printed In the USA

Author
Braxton R. Meeks
agent@bepublished.biz

Self-Publishing Associate
Dr. Mary M. Jefferson
BePublished.Org - Chicago, IL
(972) 880-8316
www.bepublished.org

Recycled Paper Encouraged.

Table of Contents

$

(more)

TOC *(cont'd)* $

(###)

FAST MONEY EASY MONEY

PROVEN
SYSTEMS THAT ARE
TIME TESTED AND
WILL WORK IN
EMERGING
ECONOMIES
UTILIZING AI
TECH

Introduction

Money has a way of telling the truth about people — what they fear, what they value, what they're willing to risk, and what they secretly believe about themselves. For some, money is a tool. For others, it's a lifeline. And for many, it's a dream just out of reach, always close enough to imagine but never close enough to touch. We live in a world where a person can work forty years and still retire with nothing, while another person can make a single strategic decision and change the entire direction of their life. The difference between the two isn't luck. It isn't magic. And it isn't unfairness. The difference is knowledge — the kind nobody teaches, the kind too many people never learn, and the kind that separates those who chase money from those who attract it.

This book was born out of a simple truth: **money does not behave the same way for everyone.** There are people who grind all day, exhausted, stressed, and still broke. And there are people who move differently — people whose effort produces multiplied results, whose actions seem to open doors faster, whose decisions create money that does not require their constant presence. These two worlds often exist right next to each other, two realities living on the same street, sometimes in the same family. But their outcomes are miles apart.

Why?

Because there are only two paths people take when they don't inherit wealth: **Fast Money** and **Easy Money.** They are not the same. They don't produce the same life. And depending on the mindset behind them, either path can become a blessing or a trap.

In these pages, you will meet two couples. Two stories. Two approaches. Two outcomes.

One couple represents **Fast Money** — the urgent, risky, high-adrenaline, high-pressure pursuit of immediate financial gain. Fast money is seductive. It feels good. It looks good. It moves quickly. It promises relief even faster than it delivers results. People chase fast money because their circumstances demand speed, or because their pride does. When life hits hard, the need for fast cash can override caution, planning, and long-term thinking. And while fast money can feel like salvation, it can also become a cage made of gold dust — shiny, tempting, and ultimately impossible to hold onto.

The other couple represents **Easy Money** — not effortless money, not free money, but **smart money**, the kind created by systems, strategy, leverage, and intentionality. Easy money flows because it has structure. It grows because it has direction. It repeats because the person who built it understood the difference between working to survive and working to multiply. Easy money isn't slow. It simply moves with purpose instead of panic. And when built correctly, easy money leads to stability, opportunity, and eventually, wealth.

Between these two stories, you will not receive theories, opinions, or wishful thinking. You will witness reality — the emotional, financial, relational, and practical consequences of how people handle money. You will see how beliefs shape behavior, how behavior shapes outcomes, and how the smallest decisions can change everything.

But this book does not stop at storytelling. After the lives and lessons of both couples unfold, you will step into the **blueprint section** — the practical, unfiltered, step-by-step instructions on how to make money, keep money, grow money, and build a life where wealth is not an accident but an expectation. You will learn the systems, the strategies, the habits, and the actions that separate those who talk about abundance from those who consistently live in it.

$

Why This Book Is Different

Most financial books fall into one of two categories:

1. **Motivational hype** that makes you feel good but teaches you nothing.
2. **Dry financial instruction** that teaches everything except the part that matters most: how to apply it in real life.

This book refuses to live in either category.

You will get the emotion, the humanity, the relatable struggle — because money is personal and pretending it isn't keeps people broke. You will also get the structure, the clarity, the precision, and the no-nonsense guidance — because motivation without direction is useless, and direction without motivation rarely gets followed.

I am combining both. The stories keep you invested. The lessons keep you alert. The blueprint keeps you equipped. The steps keep you accountable. And together, they keep you moving toward wealth.

$$\$$

A Truth That Often Goes Untold

Most people don't need another job. They need a new **strategy.** Most don't need more hours. They need **better systems.** Most don't need to sacrifice their lives. They need to **redirect their energy.** Most don't need people to tell them to "work harder." They've already been working hard their entire lives. What they need is someone to show them **how to make money work for them.**

The couples in this book illustrate the gap between effort and outcome. They represent millions of people — people who want more, who deserve more, who try harder than the world gives them credit for. Their stories will show you how easy it is to slip into the trap of fast money and how possible it is to climb your way into the stability of easy money. And more importantly, they will show you that no matter where you stand today, wealth is not out of reach. Not for you. Not anymore.

$

The Weight of Money and the Freedom of Mastery

Money affects everything — relationships, opportunities, confidence, health, happiness, safety, dreams. When money is scarce, life becomes small, cramped, filled with anxiety and urgency. When money flows, life expands. Options multiply. Peace grows. And a person who once made choices based on fear begins making choices based on purpose.

This book is not promising that money will solve every problem. But it will absolutely solve the problems caused by **not** having it.

And for too long, people have been taught to fear money, distrust money, judge money, or settle for just enough of it. That ends here. The couples you meet will show you what money can do to people who fear it and what it can do for people who learn to respect it, understand it, and master it.

$

What You Will Learn by the Time You Finish This Book

By the final page, you will know:

- The emotional and psychological triggers that lead people toward fast money
- The habits and behaviors that quietly sabotage wealth
- The patterns that separate temporary success from lasting success
- The specific steps anyone can take to create easy, repeatable streams of income
- How to build wealth without stress, burnout, or sacrificing your relationships

- How to create systems that generate money even when you aren't actively working
- How to shift from survival thinking to wealth thinking
- How to avoid the traps that destroy financial progress
- How to make money in ways that align with who you are
- How to transition from fast money to easy money
- How to build wealth that lasts and grows

And unlike most books, you won't be told "what" to do without being taught "how." For every lesson, there will be exact steps, practical instructions, and clear directions. No vagueness. No guessing. No ambiguity. You will leave with a plan. You will leave with tools. You will leave with understanding. And you will leave with the confidence to execute.

$

Why the Combination of Story + Strategy Works

People learn through example. People change through understanding. People grow through connection.

When you watch someone else succeed or fail, something powerful happens inside you. You gain insight without paying the cost of the mistake. You gain wisdom without enduring the consequence. You gain clarity without losing anything in the process.

That is what these stories deliver.

The fast-money couple will show you the adrenaline, the excitement, the illusion of control, the strain it places on relationships, and the consequences that follow quick decisions made with desperation or ego. Their journey is not a warning — it is a mirror. And many will see themselves in it.

The easy-money couple will show you the peace that structure brings, the freedom that systems create, the way money grows quietly when it is built correctly, and the financial confidence that comes from knowing you are no longer living at the mercy of chance. Their journey is not an ideal — it is a model. And many will see who they can become through it.

And when both stories have been fully told, the book will shift into something far more powerful: Guidance that transforms potential into profit.

$

This Book Is a Doorway

Every person has at least one moment in their life that changes everything — a conversation, a decision, a realization, a risk, a turning point. Something small that leads to something big. Something unexpected that unlocks something necessary.

For many, this book will be that moment.

Not because it contains secrets, but because it contains truth. Not because it offers shortcuts, but because it offers clarity. Not because it promises riches, but because it teaches reality. There is no magic here. No tricks. No hype. Just wisdom, strategy, and the courage to apply them.

$

What I Want for You

Before you take another step into these pages, I want you to understand something clearly:

You are capable of wealth. You are not too late. You have not missed your chance. You are not excluded from abundance. You are not disqualified by your mistakes.

You are not trapped by your circumstances.

Wealth is not reserved for the lucky. It is not reserved for the connected. It is not reserved for the privileged.

It is reserved for the prepared.

And preparation begins now.

This book was written to change the way you see money, the way you move with money, and the way money responds to you. Once you understand the differences between fast money and easy money — once you see how these two energies shape lives — you will be able to choose your path with clarity instead of confusion.

There is no shame in wanting to live better. There is no guilt in wanting more. There is no apology needed for wanting wealth.

You are not here to suffer. You are not here to scrape by. You are not here to merely survive.

You are here to live. You are here to grow. You are here to establish a legacy that outlives you.

That is why this book exists. That is why these pages matter. That is why your story is about to change.

Because after this introduction, you will not only witness the difference between fast money and easy money — you will understand how to build a life where money flows toward you with purpose, direction, and stability.

Let's begin.

PART I

THE

FAST MONEY

PATH

Chapter 1
Meet the Fast Money Couple

Fast money doesn't arrive in a vacuum. It enters a life that has already been stretched thin.

Before the Fast Money Couple ever chased speed, risk, or quick wins, they were simply two people trying to do what most people are told will work: get educated enough, work hard enough, stay responsible, and trust that consistency would eventually lead to stability. They didn't grow up believing shortcuts were the answer. They grew up believing effort mattered.

That belief is what makes their story so important. Let's take a moment to focus on Jordan and Leila.

$

Where They Came From

Neither of them came from wealth. There were no trust funds, no safety nets, no inherited assets quietly working in the background. Their families worked. Hard. Long hours. Physical jobs. Salaried jobs that never seemed to stretch far enough. Money was discussed, but rarely understood. It was something to manage, something to worry about, something that was never quite sufficient.

From an early age, both Jordan and Leila learned the same lesson: *money equals security*. When money was tight, stress filled the room. When money was short, arguments followed. When money was absent, choices disappeared. That connection never left them.

He learned to equate money with responsibility. He watched the pressure it put on the adults around him and absorbed the idea that providing wasn't optional — it was proof of worth. Falling short financially wasn't just inconvenient; it was personal failure.

She learned to equate money with freedom. She saw how lack of money trapped people in routines they hated and situations they couldn't escape. She dreamed of a life that felt lighter, easier, less constrained by constant calculation.

They didn't talk about these beliefs when they met. They didn't have to. They felt familiar to each other in a way that didn't need explanation.

$$\$$$

Early Ambition and Shared Dreams

When they first built their life together, money wasn't abundant — but hope was. They talked about the future constantly. About what they would do "once things settled down." About the kind of life they wanted once they were no longer scrambling.

Leila and Jordan believed in progress. They believed that each year would be better than the last. They believed that patience would pay off.

And for a while, it seemed like it was.

They advanced in their careers. Their income increased incrementally. They checked off the boxes society said mattered: stability, responsibility, adulthood. From the outside, they were doing fine. From the inside, they were constantly calculating — running numbers, timing expenses, juggling obligations.

There was no margin. No buffer. No room for error.

Any unexpected cost required sacrifice elsewhere. Any setback erased months of effort. They weren't failing, but they weren't advancing either. They were treading water in deeper and deeper waves.

$

The Financial Strain Beneath the Surface

What wore them down wasn't poverty. It was *fragility*.

They lived in a constant state of near-enough. Enough to survive, enough to function, enough to appear stable. But not enough to feel safe. Not enough to breathe.

They couldn't miss a paycheck. They couldn't afford extended downtime. They couldn't make a mistake.

Every decision carried weight. Every purchase required justification. Every plan had to be double-checked against the budget. Over time, that kind of mental load erodes optimism.

They didn't talk openly about how heavy it felt. They were proud. Capable. Responsible. Admitting struggle felt like admitting weakness. So instead, Leila and Jordan internalized it.

He took on more pressure, believing it was his role to fix things. She reassured him, believing optimism was the glue holding them together. But reassurance doesn't erase reality. It only delays confrontation with it.

$

The Shift From Patience to Pressure

Patience works best when progress is visible. When time passes without meaningful change, patience starts to feel like denial.

They began to notice how long they had been "almost there." How many years they had been preparing for a future that never seemed to arrive. They were older now. Responsibilities had grown. The window for risk felt smaller, not larger.

What once felt like a reasonable pace began to feel unacceptable.

They didn't want extravagance. They wanted control. They wanted margin. They wanted proof that their effort mattered.

This is where fast money begins to whisper.

$

Exposure to Fast Money Thinking

They didn't stumble into fast money blindly. They were exposed to it gradually, through conversations, stories, and examples. Someone they knew made in a month what they made in a year. Someone else flipped an opportunity and walked away with instant profit.

At first, they dismissed it. Then they questioned it. Then they studied it.

Fast money didn't look reckless from the outside. It looked *smart*. Strategic. Confident. Efficient. The people earning it seemed to move with certainty. Leila and Jordan spoke a different language — about leverage, timing, opportunity, risk.

Compared to their own slow grind, fast money looked like evolution.

They began asking themselves uncomfortable questions:

Why are we working this hard for this little return?
Why does doing everything "right" still feel like falling behind?
Why does stability cost so much and give so little?

Fast money offered a compelling answer: *Because you're playing the wrong game.*

$

Why Fast Money Made Sense to Them

Fast money wasn't about greed for them. It was about math.

They ran the numbers. They compared timelines. They imagined what could happen if even a portion of their income came in faster, larger chunks. One good win could erase debt. Two could build savings. Three could change everything.

Speed felt logical.

Why wait decades for compound growth when you could accelerate the process? Why accept incremental improvement when bold moves produced immediate results? Why cling to security that barely existed when risk promised relief?

Fast money felt like realism, not recklessness.

$

The Belief That "Fast Money Is The Only Real Money"

This belief didn't appear overnight.

It formed slowly, reinforced by experience and observation. Slow money had failed them. Traditional paths hadn't delivered. Consistency hadn't created security.

Fast money, on the other hand, *worked* — at least initially. When they tested it, it responded. Effort turned into cash quickly. Decisions had immediate consequences. Results were tangible.

They began to see slow money as inefficient. Outdated. Designed for a world that no longer existed. In their eyes, slow money required too much time for too little return.

Fast money felt honest. It didn't pretend. It didn't delay gratification. It didn't require blind faith.

They told themselves they were just being practical.

$

Emotional Validation and Identity Shift

The first real fast-money win changed more than their finances — it changed their identity.

For the first time, Leila and Jordan felt powerful. Capable in a new way. Smart in a way that wasn't validated by titles or resumes but by results. Money arrived quickly, and with it came confidence.

They walked differently. They spoke differently. They planned differently.

Fast money validated what they had suspected all along: that they weren't failing because they lacked ability, but because they had been trapped in a slow system.

That realization was intoxicating.

$

The Pressure to Keep Winning

Fast money doesn't just reward success — it demands continuity. Once they experienced momentum, stopping felt impossible. Slowing down felt dangerous. Each win raised expectations. Each loss increased urgency.

They began to feel responsible not just for earning, but for maintaining pace. Fast money became their proof of competence. Losing it felt like regression.

The stress increased, but so did the stakes. Jordan and Leila told themselves it was temporary. That once they stabilized, they would slow down. That once they "caught up," they would be careful.

Fast money always promises later.

$

Relationship Dynamics Under Speed

Speed changes relationships. Decisions are made faster than conversations can keep up. One partner pushes forward while the other tries to manage risk. Misalignment grows quietly.

They still loved each other. They still wanted the same future. But they began to differ on how much risk was acceptable, how much pressure was sustainable, how far was too far. Fast money magnified every difference.

What used to be small disagreements became loaded. What used to be shared optimism became competing anxieties. Money wasn't just a tool anymore — it was a test.

$

What This Couple Represents

The Fast Money Couple is not extreme. Jordan and Leila are common. They represent people who did what they were told and still felt behind. People who tried patience and were punished by time. People who didn't want excess but couldn't survive on almost.

They represent the moment when ambition collides with reality — and chooses speed. Their belief that fast money is the only real money did not come from ignorance. It came from experience. From years of slow returns, fragile stability, and deferred dreams. And that belief makes sense — until its consequences unfold.

This chapter is not a warning or a condemnation. It is context. Because before fast money becomes dangerous, it always feels justified. Logical. Necessary. Their story begins here — not with recklessness, but with hope sharpened by pressure. And pressure changes everything.

Chapter 2
The Rise: Their Fast Money Strategies

Fast money doesn't begin with recklessness. It begins with movement.

After their first taste of speed, the Fast Money Couple didn't suddenly abandon logic or planning. They became *more* focused, not less. What changed was their tolerance for waiting. Slow outcomes no longer felt responsible — they felt negligent.

If time was the enemy, speed was the weapon.

$

How They First Started Making Fast Money

Their entry point wasn't dramatic. It was opportunistic.

They didn't quit their jobs or gamble everything on a single move. Instead, they layered fast money on top of their existing structure, testing it like an experiment. A side hustle here. A flip there. A calculated risk they believed they could unwind if necessary.

The key difference between what they had done before and what they were doing now was **compression**. Time collapsed. Results arrived faster. Feedback was immediate.

They started by identifying inefficiencies — places where effort or insight could be exchanged for cash quickly. Reselling undervalued items. Short-term arbitrage. Small investments with quick turnaround. Nothing glamorous. Nothing that looked dangerous on paper.

But it worked.

The first profits weren't huge, but they were fast. Money earned in days instead of months. That speed alone felt revolutionary. It didn't matter that the absolute amount was modest; what mattered was that the system responded *immediately*.

For the first time, effort wasn't deferred.

$

Side Hustles That Turned Into Accelerators

What began as side hustles quickly became engines.

Jordan and Leila learned how to stack small wins — how to keep capital moving instead of letting it sit. They reinvested aggressively, convinced that idle money was wasted time. Each cycle tightened their process. Each success sharpened their instincts.

They didn't think of themselves as hustlers. They thought of themselves as optimizers.

Their days changed. Evenings became strategic sessions. Weekends turned into execution windows. Conversations revolved around opportunity, not exhaustion. They felt alive in a way they hadn't felt in years.

Fast money brought clarity. When something worked, they doubled down. When something failed, they moved on without sentiment. Speed rewarded decisiveness. Hesitation cost money.

This wasn't chaos. It was momentum.

$

Flipping: Turning Insight Into Cash

Flipping became one of their favorite strategies because it embodied everything they believed about money. Buy low. Sell fast. Capture value before time eroded it.

They trained themselves to see opportunity everywhere. What others overlooked, they evaluated. What others hesitated on, they acted on. Leila and Jordan didn't need perfection — they needed *movement*.

Flipping taught them that value was relative and timing was everything. A deal wasn't good or bad in isolation; it was good or bad *right now*. This mindset carried into every area of their financial life.

Money stopped feeling scarce. It started feeling *fluid*.

$

High-Risk Plays and Calculated Danger

As confidence grew, so did appetite.

High-risk plays entered the picture gradually. At first, they justified them as asymmetric bets — limited downside, massive upside. They told themselves they were being strategic, not reckless.

And sometimes, they were right.

A bold move paid off. A leveraged position turned into a windfall. A risk others avoided became their advantage. Each win reinforced the belief that courage was rewarded and caution was punished.

Jordan and Leila began to trust their instincts more than conventional wisdom. They dismissed warnings as fear-based thinking from people who had never moved fast enough to win big.

Fast money didn't just change their finances — it changed who they listened to.

$

Leveraged Moves and the Illusion of Control

Leverage is seductive because it feels like intelligence multiplied.

Using other people's money, borrowed time, or future earnings allowed them to scale faster than their actual resources would normally permit. They saw leverage as efficiency — why wait when you could amplify?

Early leverage worked. That's what made it dangerous. Every successful leveraged move reinforced the illusion of control.

Jordan and Leila believed they understood the game well enough to manage risk. They believed they could exit before consequences arrived.

Leverage didn't feel heavy yet. It felt empowering.

$

The Emotional and Psychological Mindset Behind Moving Fast

Speed reshaped their inner world. They became alert, energized, hyper-focused. Their brains adjusted to quick feedback loops. Dopamine spikes followed every win. Even losses felt stimulating — problems to solve, puzzles to crack.

Fast money made them feel competent in a way slow money never had. There was no waiting for approval. No delayed validation. The market responded instantly.

They felt chosen. This mindset bred confidence, and confidence bred decisiveness. Decisiveness bred results. The loop reinforced itself. Leila and Jordan told themselves they had finally cracked the code.

$

Early Wins and the Seduction of Success

The early wins came in waves. One success funded the next. One profit erased an old stress. One month outperformed an entire year of their previous income trajectory. They didn't just make money — they made *progress*.

They paid off lingering debts. They padded accounts that had never stayed full. Jordan and Leila upgraded their environment, not extravagantly, but noticeably. Small comforts that felt earned rather than indulgent.

The psychological relief was profound. Money stopped being a constant anxiety and became a tool. A lever. A scoreboard. They felt lighter. More capable. More aligned with their ambitions.

$

Lifestyle Changes: Subtle but Significant

Their lifestyle didn't explode overnight. It evolved.

They allowed themselves things they had postponed for years — better food, better experiences, occasional spontaneity. They no longer calculated every decision down to the dollar. Time became more flexible. Options multiplied.

Leila and Jordan still worked hard, but it felt different. Effort felt purposeful rather than obligatory. Long hours felt justified when rewards were immediate. They weren't rich — but they were no longer trapped.

$

Identity Shift: Becoming "People Who Move Fast"

Perhaps the most significant change wasn't financial — it was identity. They stopped seeing themselves as workers and started seeing themselves as operators. People who acted. People who moved before others noticed opportunity.

This identity felt earned. Validated. Dangerous to lose. They told themselves a story: *We're not lucky — we're decisive.* And stories shape behavior.

$

Impact on Their Relationship

At first, fast money strengthened their bond.

Jordan and Leila were a team. Strategists. Co-conspirators in success. They shared victories intimately because few others understood the pressure or the pace.

Late nights became brainstorming sessions. Wins were celebrated privately, losses dissected together. There was intimacy in shared risk. They felt aligned.

But speed also compressed communication. Decisions happened quickly. Assumptions replaced discussion. One partner often moved faster than the other emotionally, even if they agreed intellectually.

Small tensions were postponed because momentum felt more important than resolution. Fast money doesn't slow down for conversations.

$

Social Perception and External Validation

Others noticed. Friends commented on their confidence. Family noticed changes in tone, posture, optimism. Some admired them. Others questioned them. A few quietly envied them.

Validation came from unexpected places. People asked for advice. Sought insight. Treated them like experts. This external recognition amplified their internal belief: *We're doing something right.*

Jordan and Leila became more guarded about setbacks and more vocal about wins. Not out of arrogance — but protection. Success felt fragile, and they didn't want doubt contaminating momentum.

$

The Growing Commitment to Speed

By now, fast money wasn't just a strategy — it was a commitment. They structured their lives around opportunity. They optimized schedules for responsiveness. They stayed alert, connected, ready.

Slow money felt intolerable by comparison. Waiting felt like waste. Stability felt like stagnation.

They told themselves this phase was temporary — that once they reached a certain threshold, they would slow down, diversify, secure. But fast money always raises the threshold.

$

What This Rise Really Represents

The rise of the Fast Money Couple is not about greed or irresponsibility. It's about relief. Relief from pressure. Relief from fragility. Relief from waiting.

Fast money gave Jordan and Leila something slow money never had: proof that change was possible *now*. That proof is powerful. It reshapes values. It rewrites rules. It convinces people they have finally outgrown limitations.

And that's why fast money is seductive — not because it promises luxury, but because it delivers *immediacy*.

This chapter is the ascent — the phase where everything works just well enough to justify everything that follows.

Because before fast money reveals its cost, it rewards belief.

And belief, when reinforced by early success, is the most dangerous asset of all.

Chapter 3
The Cost of Fast Money

Fast money always sends the bill later.

It doesn't announce itself as a cost. It arrives quietly, disguised as fatigue, tension, impatience, and the constant feeling that you can't slow down without losing ground. At first, the Fast Money Couple didn't recognize what was happening. Leila and Jordan were still winning often enough to believe everything was under control.

But control is fragile when speed is mandatory.

$

Stress as a Constant Companion

The first real cost was stress — not the obvious kind, but the low-grade, ever-present pressure that never fully turned off.

Fast money required attention. Constant attention.

Opportunities didn't wait. Markets didn't pause. Deals expired. Windows closed. Alerts pinged at all hours. Every moment away felt like a potential loss. Even relaxation carried guilt.

They told themselves the stress was temporary. That this was the price of acceleration. That everyone who "made it" paid this toll on the way up. But stress compounds when it has no off switch.

Sleep became lighter. Thoughts raced longer. Decisions followed them into bed. Even wins failed to bring peace because the next move always waited behind it. Fast money doesn't allow satisfaction — it only allows momentum.

$

Instability Hidden Behind Highs

On the surface, things still looked good. Money was coming in. Sometimes a lot of it. But the timing was unpredictable. Income arrived in spikes instead of streams. A great week could erase the anxiety of the previous two — until the next dry spell reignited it.

They lived in a constant state of recalibration.

Budgets stopped making sense because averages didn't reflect reality. Planning felt pointless when numbers swung wildly. They learned to live reactively — adjusting spending, delaying commitments, reshuffling priorities based on what just happened.

Instability became normalized. They weren't broke, but they were never settled. Fast money creates the illusion of abundance while quietly eroding predictability. And predictability is what allows people to rest.

$

Burnout Disguised as Ambition

Burnout doesn't arrive suddenly. It creeps in disguised as drive. Jordan and Leila pushed through exhaustion because the rewards were immediate. They told themselves they could rest later — after the next deal, the next win, the next milestone.

But the milestones kept moving.

Their energy began to fracture. Motivation spiked only when money was on the line. Joy outside of work dulled. Conversations circled back to money even when they tried to escape it.

Fast money trained their nervous systems to stay activated. Adrenaline replaced balance. Urgency replaced rhythm. And eventually, their bodies started keeping score.

$

Inconsistency and the Emotional Whiplash

Fast money isn't just inconsistent financially — it's emotionally volatile.

High highs followed by sharp drops. Confidence surged, then collapsed. Wins made them feel invincible; losses made them question everything.

Their self-worth began tracking performance.

When things worked, they felt smart, capable, ahead. When things failed, they felt exposed, foolish, behind. There was no neutral ground.

They were either winning or scrambling. This emotional whiplash drained them more than the work itself. The constant recalibration of identity — *Am I successful or am I failing?* — became exhausting.

Fast money doesn't just test strategy. It tests emotional resilience.

$

Bad Deals: The Cost of Speed

Speed reduces margin for error.

As they moved faster, diligence suffered. Not because they didn't know better, but because time felt too expensive to spend verifying every detail.

Jordan and Leila told themselves they had good instincts. That experience had sharpened their judgment. And sometimes it had. But speed amplifies mistakes.

They entered deals that looked good at first glance but hid structural flaws. Terms were misunderstood. Assumptions went unchallenged. Optimism filled gaps where analysis should have lived.

One bad deal didn't ruin them — but it shook them. Losses that took weeks to recover erased months of gains emotionally. The sting lingered longer than the win that preceded it. Fast money forgives nothing.

$

Scams, Traps, and Predators

Where money moves fast, predators follow.

As their activity increased, so did exposure. They encountered people who spoke fluently about opportunity but vaguely about risk. Offers arrived wrapped in urgency — *limited time, exclusive access, act now.*

They missed red flags because speed rewarded trust over skepticism.

They didn't fall for everything — but they fell for enough.

Each scam wasn't just a financial hit; it was a psychological one. Embarrassment layered on top of loss. Self-doubt crept in. Trust eroded — not just in others, but in themselves.

Fast money environments thrive on momentum, and momentum is easy to manipulate.

$

Losses That Cut Deeper Than Numbers

Some losses hurt more than money. There were losses of time — months spent chasing something that went nowhere. Losses of reputation — associations with people who disappeared when things went bad. Losses of confidence — moments where their instincts failed them publicly.

Losses created hesitation, and hesitation clashed with the speed they had built their identity around. Leila and Jordan felt trapped between slowing down and risking more. Fast money doesn't prepare you for reflection — it punishes it.

$

Strain on the Relationship

At first, fast money brought them closer. Now it began to pull them apart.

Stress changed how they spoke to each other. Shorter conversations. Less patience. More assumptions. Money became a sensitive topic instead of a shared goal.

One partner began to crave stability while the other clung to momentum. Conversations turned circular. Disagreements went unresolved because slowing down felt dangerous.

They still loved each other — but love was now competing with urgency. Fast money compresses decision-making, and relationships need space to breathe.

$

Time Becomes the First Casualty

Time disappeared quietly.

Work bled into evenings. Even "off" moments were interrupted by notifications, calls, or mental calculations. Presence eroded.

Jordan and Leila were together often — but rarely fully there. Vacations felt tense. Dinners were distracted. Silence filled gaps where conversation used to live.

Fast money stole time not by force, but by necessity. When speed is survival, everything else becomes optional.

$

Health: The Unpaid Invoice

Eventually, their bodies protested.

Sleep deprivation accumulated. Stress manifested physically — headaches, fatigue, tension that never fully released. Small illnesses lingered longer. Recovery slowed.

They ignored the signs because stopping felt impossible. Health became negotiable.

Fast money taught them to trade long-term well-being for short-term gains, even when they knew better.

The irony wasn't lost on them: they were earning money faster than ever, but spending health just as quickly.

$

The Psychological Toll of Always Being "On"

Fast money requires vigilance.

Jordan and Leila stayed alert for opportunity and danger simultaneously. Their minds never rested. Even success triggered anticipation instead of peace.

They became reactive.

Calm felt unfamiliar. Stillness felt unsafe.

Fast money rewires the nervous system to expect volatility, and volatility becomes normal — even addictive.

But addiction to intensity is not resilience. It's dependency.

$

The Cracks Become Visible

Eventually, the cracks showed.

Wins no longer felt satisfying enough to justify the stress. Losses felt heavier. Fatigue dulled excitement.

The lifestyle that once felt empowering now felt demanding.

They weren't failing — but they weren't thriving either.

They realized something unsettling:
Fast money had improved their income but degraded their quality of life.

And quality of life is the reason money matters in the first place.

$

The Unspoken Question

They began asking a question they had avoided:
What happens if this pace becomes permanent?

Fast money had no built-in exit strategy. No natural slowing point. No clear transition to stability. The system they built required them to stay sharp, fast, and available indefinitely. And that realization frightened them more than any loss.

$

What This Chapter Represents

This chapter isn't a condemnation of fast money. It's a revelation.

Fast money works — but it extracts payment in ways that aren't immediately obvious. Stress replaces peace. Instability replaces safety. Speed replaces sustainability.

The Fast Money Couple didn't fail because they were reckless. They succeeded just long enough to expose the limits of acceleration without foundation. Fast money doesn't collapse suddenly. It erodes quietly. And by the time people notice the cost, they are often too invested to stop easily.

This chapter marks the turning point — not because everything falls apart, but because awareness arrives. And awareness is the beginning of every real change.

Because once you understand the true cost of fast money, you can no longer pretend speed alone is enough.

The bill has arrived. What happens next depends on whether they keep running — or finally learn how to stand still long enough to build something that lasts.

Chapter 4
What the Fast Money Couple Learns (But Too Late)

The most painful lessons are not the ones that come from failure. They are the ones that come *after success*, when you finally understand what you should have done differently — but only once the cost has already been paid.

For the Fast Money Couple, the reckoning didn't arrive as a single collapse. There was no dramatic crash, no sudden bankruptcy, no moment where everything vanished overnight. Instead, the realization arrived slowly, quietly, almost politely.

Jordan and Leila were still standing. They were still earning. But something was unmistakably wrong.

They had money — but not *wealth*. They had income — but not *security*. They had movement — but not *direction*.

And the worst part was this: the knowledge they were about to gain could have changed everything — if they had learned it sooner.

$

Fast Money Is Powerful — But Only When Treated Like a Business

Their first and biggest mistake was treating fast money like *found money* instead of *business revenue*.

Because it came quickly, they handled it casually. Because it felt temporary, they managed it emotionally. Because it didn't look like a traditional paycheck, they didn't apply traditional discipline.

Fast money felt personal. A business should never be.

They didn't separate accounts early enough. They didn't create formal systems. They didn't assign roles, schedules, or operating rules. Everything lived in their heads, their phones, their conversations.

This worked — until it didn't. Fast money behaves like a business whether you acknowledge it or not. It has cash flow cycles, expense ratios, risk exposure, tax consequences, and operational overhead. Ignoring those realities doesn't eliminate them — it just delays their impact.

By the time they realized they were running a business, they had already accumulated chaos.

$

The Tracking Mistake: "We Know Where the Money Is"

They believed they were tracking — because they were *aware*.

They checked balances. They remembered wins. They mentally noted losses. They could estimate roughly how much they had made in a good month.

What they didn't do was *document reality*.

No detailed records. No categorized expenses. No profit-and-loss statements. No clear picture of net versus gross. Fast money makes tracking feel optional because results are immediate. But immediacy hides inefficiency.

Jordan and Leila were shocked when they finally added everything up. Profits were smaller than they thought. Expenses were larger. Time costs were invisible but massive.

They weren't leaking money — they were hemorrhaging clarity. Without tracking, fast money creates confidence without comprehension. And confidence without comprehension is a liability.

$

Budgeting: The Discipline They Thought Didn't Apply to Them

They believed budgeting was for people with fixed incomes.

Fast money didn't feel compatible with structure. Income was irregular. Opportunities were unpredictable. They told themselves budgeting would limit flexibility.

What they didn't realize was that *lack of budgeting was limiting survival*. They budgeted reactively — cutting when cash slowed, loosening when wins came in. This emotional budgeting kept them on edge and trained their nervous systems to respond to volatility instead of stability.

A real budget doesn't restrict opportunity — it creates runway. By the time they tried to implement one, their lifestyle had already adjusted upward. Fixed costs had increased. Obligations had multiplied. Flexibility was gone.

Fast money should have been managed with *conservative budgets built on average months*, not peak ones. But they learned that too late.

$

Taxes: The Silent Assassin of Fast Money

Nothing humbled them faster than taxes. Fast money doesn't withhold. It doesn't remind. It doesn't protect. It assumes you know what you're doing. They didn't.

At first, taxes felt abstract — something future them would handle. But fast money compounds tax exposure quickly. Each win carried an invisible liability. When the bill arrived, it wasn't just financial — it was psychological.

They hadn't planned for it. They hadn't set money aside consistently. They had already reinvested, spent, or leveraged funds that technically weren't fully theirs. Taxes turned wins into losses retroactively.

Leila and Jordan learned a hard truth: *If you don't manage taxes proactively, fast money punishes you for being successful.* Wealthy people respect taxes. Fast money chasers ignore them — until they can't.

$

Reinvesting vs. Recycling: A Critical Difference

They believed they were reinvesting. In reality, they were *recycling*. Reinvestment builds systems that generate future value. Recycling simply keeps money moving without increasing durability.

They poured money back into the next deal, the next opportunity, the next high-return promise. What they didn't do was allocate capital to infrastructure — processes, tools, protections, or assets that reduced dependency on constant effort.

Fast money kept them busy. Wealth requires leverage beyond labor. They confused activity with advancement.

True reinvestment looks boring compared to fast money. It prioritizes stability over excitement, consistency over spikes. It doesn't feel urgent — but it compounds.

By the time they recognized this, they had little to show that could operate without them.

$$\$$$

Boundaries: The Lesson That Costs the Most

Fast money erases boundaries unless you enforce them intentionally.

They didn't. Work hours blurred. Rest became conditional. Availability became constant. Every opportunity felt too important to ignore.

Jordan and Leila said yes too often — to deals, to people, to pressure. Without boundaries, fast money consumes everything: time, attention, relationships, health.

They believed boundaries would slow them down. What they didn't realize was that lack of boundaries was already slowing them — just invisibly.

Burnout wasn't a surprise. It was an inevitability.

$

Why Most Fast Money Earners Never Build True Wealth

This is the lesson that hurt the most — because it wasn't personal. It was structural.

Fast money earners don't fail because they can't earn. They fail because earning becomes the focus instead of *keeping, structuring, and protecting*.

Fast money rewards action. Wealth rewards restraint. Fast money celebrates speed. Wealth values timing. Fast money builds income. Wealth builds insulation.

The Fast Money Couple didn't lack intelligence, ambition, or work ethic. They lacked systems, patience, and early discipline.

By the time they understood the difference, their energy was depleted, their margin thin, and their enthusiasm dulled. They had spent their most powerful years chasing speed instead of building permanence.

$

The Illusion of "Later"

Their biggest mistake wasn't what they did — it was what they postponed.

They told themselves:

- We'll organize later

- We'll slow down later

- We'll stabilize once we hit X

- We'll build wealth after this phase

But fast money doesn't naturally lead to later. It creates an environment where *now* is always louder. Later never arrived.

$

The Emotional Weight of Knowing Better

Knowledge gained late carries a unique kind of pain. Jordan and Leila could see the alternate timeline clearly — the one where they tracked early, budgeted conservatively, respected taxes, reinvested strategically, and enforced boundaries.

That version of them wasn't luckier. Just earlier. Jordan and Leila didn't beat themselves up — but they did grieve.

They grieved wasted energy. They grieved unnecessary stress. They grieved years that could have compounded quietly instead of burning loudly.

$

What This Chapter Is Really About

This chapter isn't about regret — it's about revelation. Fast money is not the enemy. Unmanaged fast money is. Speed without structure doesn't lead to wealth — it leads to exhaustion.

The Fast Money Couple learned lessons that every fast money earner eventually learns. The difference is *when*.

Those who learn early convert momentum into permanence. Those who learn late spend momentum just surviving it.

This chapter exists so the reader doesn't have to learn the hard way. Because fast money can be a powerful starting point — but only if it's treated like a business from day one, governed by systems, and guided by restraint.

Otherwise, it teaches you everything you need to know — just when you no longer have the energy to use it. And that is the most expensive lesson of all.

Chapter 5
Fast Money Lessons You Can Use

Fast money is not the villain of this book Ignorance is. Speed is not the problem. Lack of structure is. Momentum is not dangerous. Unmanaged momentum is. This chapter exists for one reason: to turn fast money from a gamble into a **tool**.

The Fast Money Couple paid for their education with stress, lost time, and missed compounding. You don't have to. What follows are **practical, repeatable systems** that allow you to earn fast money *without letting it own you* — and then convert that money into real, durable wealth.

This is not theory. This is execution.

'$

PART I — HOW TO DO FAST MONEY SAFELY

Fast money becomes unsafe when it is:

- Emotional

- Untracked

- Intertwined with personal finances

- Treated as luck instead of labor

The goal is not to slow you down. The goal is to **contain the blast radius**.

Rule 1: Separate Fast Money From Life Money

This is non-negotiable.

Fast money must live in its **own ecosystem**.

Step-by-step:

1. Open a separate checking account labeled *Fast Money Ops*

2. Open a separate savings account labeled *Fast Money Taxes*

3. (Optional but smart) Open a separate business entity if volume is high

Why this matters:

- You always know what money is at risk

- Losses don't threaten rent, food, or family

- Wins don't trick you into lifestyle inflation

Fast Money Rule:
If losing it would hurt your life, it is not fast money — it is gambling.

$

Rule 2: Cap Risk Per Move (The 10% Rule)

Fast money dies when one loss wipes out ten wins.

Never risk more than 10% of your fast money capital on any single move.

If you have:

- $5,000 \rightarrow$ max risk per play = $500

- $20,000 $\rightarrow$ max risk per play = $2,000

This rule protects you from:

- Overconfidence after wins

- Emotional doubling down

- One bad deal destroying momentum

Fast money is a volume game, not a hero play.

$

Rule 3: Define the Exit Before the Entry

Every fast money move needs **three numbers written down before execution**:

1. Entry amount

2. Exit profit target

3. Maximum acceptable loss

If you cannot define all three, you do not have a strategy — you have a hope.

Example:

- Entry: $2,000

- Exit Win: $2,600

- Exit Loss: $1,700

No improvising mid-play.
No "just one more day."
No ego.

Rule 4: Timebox Your Fast Money

Fast money should not consume your entire life.

Set strict windows:

- Example: 90 minutes per day

- Or: 3 fixed sessions per week

When the time is over, you stop.

This prevents:

- Burnout

- Obsession

- Poor decisions made while exhausted

Fast money thrives on focus — not obsession.

$

PART II — FAST MONEY SYSTEMS THAT WORK

Below are **categories**, not promises. Each requires skill, discipline, and respect for risk.

System 1: Flipping & Arbitrage (Speed + Insight)

This is the safest entry point.

Steps:

1. Choose ONE category (electronics, tools, collectibles, furniture, tickets, etc.)

2. Study market prices for 30 days

3. Buy only when you can resell within 14 days

4. Never hold inventory emotionally

Checklist Before Buying:

- Can I resell this within 2 weeks?

- Is demand proven?

- Is my profit at least 20% after fees?

- Can I absorb a full loss without stress?

$

System 2: Service Compression (Fast Cash for Solved Problems)

This is fast money without inventory.

Examples:

- Cleanup

- Setup

- Fixing

- Transport

- Organization

- Automation for small businesses

Formula:

Take something slow or annoying → make it fast → charge for relief

Key Rule:

You charge for **speed and certainty**, not hours.

$

System 3: Opportunity Brokering

You don't need capital — you need connections.

Steps:

1. Identify people with problems

2. Identify people with solutions

3. Get paid for the introduction

Script Example:

"I can connect you with someone who solves this problem. If it works, my fee is X."

No delivery. No inventory. No overhead.

$

PART III — HOW TO REINVEST FAST PROFITS INTO STABLE WEALTH

Fast money is **fuel**, not the destination.

The 50/30/20 Allocation Rule

Every fast money profit gets split immediately:

- **50% → Wealth Bucket**
- **30% → Fast Money Reinvestment**
- **20% → Taxes & Protection**

This prevents the #1 mistake fast earners make: recycling everything back into risk.

$

What Goes Into the Wealth Bucket

Wealth money must do one of three things:

1. Reduce risk

2. Create predictability

3. Compound quietly

Examples:

- Emergency fund (6 months expenses)

- Debt elimination

- Long-term investments

- Business infrastructure

- Cash reserves

If it doesn't reduce future stress, it's not wealth — it's consumption.

$

Turning Speed Into Stability

The moment fast money funds:

- predictable income

- protected assets

- time freedom

…it has done its job.

Fast money is successful **only if it eventually makes itself unnecessary**.

$

PART IV — LEGAL & FINANCIAL PROTECTION

Fast money without protection is borrowed time.

Basic Legal Safeguards

At higher volume:

- Form an LLC or equivalent

- Separate business and personal accounts

- Use contracts — even simple ones

Rule:
If money is involved, clarity must be written.

$

Tax Protection Checklist

- Track every dollar earned

- Set aside 20–30% immediately

- File quarterly estimates if required

- Hire a professional once volume grows

Taxes don't punish income. They punish disorganization.

$

Insurance & Liability Awareness

Ask yourself:

- If this goes wrong, who pays?

- Can I absorb that cost?

- Is insurance cheaper than the risk?

Fast money doesn't excuse avoidable exposure.

$

PART V — EXACT SCRIPTS & TEMPLATES

Opportunity Decline Script

"This looks interesting, but it doesn't fit my risk rules. I'm going to pass."

Say it without apology.

$

Boundary Script

"I don't make financial decisions under time pressure."

Urgency is often manipulation.

$

Fast Money Daily Checklist

- Did I track today's activity?

- Did I respect my risk limits?

- Did I stop at my time boundary?

- Did I separate profit immediately?

If the answer is no to any — pause.

$

Weekly Review Template

- Total invested:

- Total profit:

- Total loss:

- Lessons learned:

- One improvement next week:

This turns chaos into data.

$

PART VI — THE MINDSET THAT MAKES FAST MONEY WORK

Fast money must be governed by **humility**.

You are not special. Markets do not care. Luck exists. Losses will happen.

Your edge is not brilliance — it is discipline.

- **Three Mental Rules**

1. No single win proves anything

2. No single loss defines you

3. Survival is success

The goal is not to be right — it is to **still be standing**.

$

WHY THIS CHAPTER MATTERS

Fast money is neither good nor bad.
It is **amplifying**.

It amplifies:

- discipline or chaos

- wisdom or ego

- structure or stress

Used correctly, fast money becomes a **launchpad**. Used carelessly, it becomes a treadmill. The Fast Money Couple learned these lessons after paying full price. You don't have to.

If you respect speed, contain risk, and convert profits into permanence, fast money can be one of the most powerful tools you ever touch.

But only if you remember this: **Fast money is rented. Wealth is owned.** The rest of this book will show you how to make the transition — before speed starts charging interest.

PART II:
THE EASY MONEY PATH

Chapter 6
Meet The Easy Money Couple

.In the world of wealth creation, there are those who chase adrenaline and immediate wins, and there are those who quietly construct systems that generate stability, freedom, and long-term growth. The Easy Money Couple belongs firmly in the second category. Their story is less flashy but more enduring, and understanding their journey is critical to grasping the balance between fast and easy money.

This chapter introduces their backgrounds, motivations, financial struggles, and mindset. We'll explore why they prefer **steady, predictable income streams** over high-risk, high-reward schemes and why their approach has allowed them to enjoy both **financial security and personal peace**. We'll also highlight actionable strategies you can implement in your own life, including ways to leverage AI and technology — even in emerging economies — to build easy money systems effectively.

$

Who They Are: Background and Early Life

Unlike the Fast Money Couple, whose drive was born from urgency and necessity, the Easy Money Couple's approach stems from **discipline, observation, and long-term thinking**.

- **Alex and Maya**, both in their late thirties, grew up in modest households. Alex's family prioritized education and savings, while Maya's upbringing emphasized financial independence and entrepreneurship. Early experiences with small failures — like a poorly managed small business venture during college — taught them the importance of structure, planning, and risk management.

- They both worked traditional jobs initially, gaining practical experience in finance, project management, and marketing. These roles provided them with skill sets they would later leverage into passive and automated income systems.

Their early exposure to money was cautious. They **saw the stress, conflict, and instability** caused by reckless financial decisions in their families and communities. This shaped a mindset centered on **stability, predictability, and systems**, rather than quick wins.

$

Motivations: Why Easy Money?

The Easy Money Couple is motivated by three primary desires:

1. **Freedom of Time:** They value personal autonomy over adrenaline-driven wealth. Their goal is not just to have money but to control how they spend their hours.

2. **Reduced Stress and Predictability:** Consistency in income and lifestyle protects relationships, mental health, and long-term plans.

3. **Sustainable Growth:** They recognize that wealth is not just about accumulation but also about compounding. Every dollar they save,

invest, or automate is a building block for the future.

For Alex and Maya, the idea of working day-to-day for fleeting gains was less appealing than **creating systems that generate income without constant attention**. Their approach is methodical: slow but sure, with compounding results over months and years rather than hours or weeks.

$

Financial Struggles and Lessons Learned

Even the Easy Money Couple faced obstacles. Early in their journey, they experienced:

- **Overextension in side projects:** Without clear systems, their first passive income attempts failed.

- **Miscalculated investments:** Initial attempts at real estate and small online ventures led to losses due to poor market research.

- **Time management challenges:** Balancing jobs, family, and early entrepreneurial attempts tested their patience and resolve.

What sets them apart is their **reflection and learning**. After each setback, they refined their methods, documenting every process, testing small before scaling, and using technology to eliminate manual labor.

$

Their Mindset: Long-Term Thinking

A key differentiator is mindset. Unlike fast money earners, the Easy Money Couple does not chase the next "big thing" without preparation. Their philosophy includes:

- **Patience is productive:** They embrace slow growth as a tool, not a limitation.

- **Systems > Effort:** Repetition without process is wasted energy. They focus on creating workflows and automations that function independently.

- **Decision Economy:** Every decision has a cost in time, energy, and risk. They minimize unnecessary choices.

- **Learning from the Fast Money Couple:** They observe fast money strategies and integrate the lessons where useful, without compromising stability.

$

Practical Lessons from Their Early Actions

Even early on, Alex and Maya were applying principles that readers can adopt today.

1. **Documenting Every Process:** From financial tracking to client communication, they created step-by-step guides.

2. **Leveraging Technology:** Even in emerging economies, they used AI-assisted tools to automate tasks — like scheduling social media, generating content for digital products, and tracking investments.

3. **Small, Repeatable Wins:** Instead of aiming for massive profits, they focused on creating **consistent, modest income streams** that compound over time.

4. **Separation of Accounts and Goals:** Each income source had a designated purpose: emergency fund, reinvestment, or lifestyle enhancement.

$

AI and Technology in Emerging Economies

One of the most exciting aspects of the Easy Money approach is that **technology levels the playing field**, even in regions with fewer financial resources. Alex and Maya implemented:

- **AI-Powered Investment Tracking:** Using AI algorithms to track stock and crypto investments, optimize portfolios, and provide alerts on market opportunities.

- **Digital Product Creation:** AI tools generate ebooks, courses, and templates that can be sold globally, providing passive income with minimal overhead.

- **Automated Customer Service & Marketing:** Chatbots and AI email automation manage client engagement for their online businesses, freeing time for strategic decisions.

- **Micro-Task Monetization:** AI platforms identify local opportunities for tasks that can generate consistent income, such as image labeling, translation, or transcription.

In emerging economies, these strategies allow individuals to **build easy money systems with minimal capital**, scaling faster than traditional methods.

$$\$$$

Lifestyle and Relationship Benefits

The Easy Money Couple enjoys more than just financial stability:

- **Peace of Mind:** Predictable income reduces stress, allowing for more focus on health, relationships, and personal growth.

- **Time Flexibility:** They can choose when and how to work, aligning their lives around family and personal interests.

- **Relationship Harmony:** Shared financial philosophy reduces conflict, as both partners understand and follow the same systems.

- **Continuous Growth:** Their income streams are designed to increase gradually over time, giving a sense of accomplishment and security simultaneously.

$

Key Takeaways for Readers

- **Start small, but systemize everything:** Focus on consistency and repeatability.

- **Use technology and AI strategically:** Automation multiplies impact while reducing effort.

- **Focus on income streams, not "quick wins":** Slow and steady builds wealth without stress.

- **Document and teach:** Make your systems reproducible for partners, employees, or even your future self.

- **Balance patience with opportunity awareness:** The best easy money earners know when to integrate fast money lessons.

$

Action Steps for the Reader

1. Identify **1–2 potential passive income streams** you can start this month.

2. Document the process for each: steps, tools, and expected outcomes.

3. Research **AI and automation tools** that can reduce effort (e.g., ChatGPT, MidJourney, AI-based social media managers).

4. Allocate **small initial capital** — even $50–$100 — to test automation or digital product ideas.

5. Track progress weekly and refine systems before scaling.

$

Conclusion of Chapter 6

Alex and Maya represent a mindset and methodology that anyone can replicate, no matter where they live. They teach us that wealth is **built by systems, patience, and discipline**, not by chasing excitement.

In emerging economies, this approach is even more powerful, because the **right AI and technology tools allow small investments of time and money to generate disproportionate results**.

By understanding their story, motivations, and methods, readers are equipped to begin constructing **their own easy money foundation**, one step at a time.

Chapter 7
Their Easy Money Systems

While Chapter 6 introduced the Easy Money Couple and their mindset, Chapter 7 dives deep into **how they create and maintain income streams that work quietly in the background**. Unlike fast money, which demands constant attention and emotional energy, easy money relies on **systems, automation, and strategic leverage**. By understanding their approach, readers can begin building their own sustainable financial engines that generate consistent wealth over time.

Alex and Maya's journey illustrates that **easy money is not passive because it requires no work — it is passive because systems do the work for you**. This chapter breaks down their methods, step by step, with practical guidance and emerging-market strategies, including AI-powered tools that make these systems scalable and low-effort.

$

The Philosophy Behind Easy Money Systems

Before exploring specific income streams, it is critical to understand **why systems matter more than effort**:

1. **Leverage multiplies impact:** Instead of trading hours for dollars, Alex and Maya design systems that create income without direct input.

2. **Consistency over adrenaline:** Slow, steady compounding beats occasional high-risk wins.

3. **Automation reduces error:** Systems that are automated or guided by AI minimize human mistakes and emotional decisions.

4. **Scalability matters:** Systems are designed to function regardless of how much income grows, ensuring sustainability.

The Easy Money Couple builds their wealth around these principles, ensuring **their lifestyle, freedom, and long-term growth remain secure**.

$

Core Easy Money Systems

Alex and Maya utilize a combination of **five primary systems**, each tailored to create stable, predictable income streams:

1. Passive Income Investments

Investing is the backbone of their system. Alex and Maya focus on assets that generate ongoing returns with minimal oversight.

Components of their investment strategy include:

- **Dividend-Paying Stocks:** Companies that regularly distribute profits.

- **High-Yield Savings or Bonds:** Low-risk instruments that provide predictable returns.

- **REITs (Real Estate Investment Trusts):** Investments in property portfolios that generate rental income.

Step-by-Step Process:

1. Allocate a fixed percentage of all income to long-term investments.

2. Use automated investment platforms to make contributions on a schedule (weekly or monthly).

3. Enable dividend reinvestment to accelerate compounding.

4. Review and rebalance portfolios quarterly, focusing on stability over speculation.

Emerging Economy Application:
Even without large capital, individuals can use micro-investment platforms to invest in ETFs, REITs, or bonds with as little as $10. AI-assisted portfolio apps analyze risk and optimize allocation automatically, ensuring small-scale investors can still benefit from compounding growth.

$

2. Digital Products and Online Businesses

Alex and Maya use digital products as scalable income systems. Unlike traditional businesses, digital products require effort upfront but function autonomously once launched.

Examples include:

- Ebooks and guides
- Online courses and workshops
- Templates for businesses or creatives
- Membership-based communities

Step-by-Step Process:

1. Identify a market need or niche where you have expertise.

2. Use AI tools to generate initial content (ChatGPT for copywriting, MidJourney for design, AI video generators for tutorials).

3. Set up automated delivery through platforms like Gumroad, Teachable, or local equivalents.

4. Automate marketing via AI social media management, email sequences, and chatbots.

Emerging Economy Application:

Digital products allow global reach from a small local investment. AI can help translate content into multiple languages, expanding potential customers without extra labor. Payment systems like PayPal, Stripe, or local mobile money platforms can automate revenue collection.

$

3. Rental and Real Estate Income

Even modest property investments provide steady cash flow. Alex and Maya strategically acquire properties with **positive cash flow potential**.

Steps to Systematize Rental Income:

1. Identify properties with high rental demand relative to cost.

2. Automate rent collection and maintenance tracking using property management software.

3. Outsource tenant communication to a trusted property manager or AI-powered virtual assistant.

4. Reinvest a portion of rental profits to scale the property portfolio.

Emerging Economy Application:
In markets with smaller property markets, short-term rentals, co-working spaces, or community-oriented rentals can provide high yields. AI tools can predict rental pricing, identify high-demand neighborhoods, and even automate listings across multiple platforms.

$

4. Automated Freelance or Service Businesses

Alex and Maya discovered early that freelance or service-based work can become partially automated. Instead of working continuously themselves, they:

- Delegate repetitive tasks to virtual assistants

- Automate scheduling, invoicing, and follow-ups

- Use AI tools to perform content creation, analytics, or reporting

Example:
A social media marketing client pays $500/month. Alex and Maya use AI to create posts, AI analytics to track engagement, and a virtual assistant to schedule content. They earn without daily involvement.

Emerging Economy Application:
Freelance marketplaces are accessible globally. AI increases efficiency, allowing people to compete internationally without hiring large teams. Even clients in small towns can receive professional-level output, while local talent earns premium income.

$

5. Long-Term Intellectual Property and Licensing

Finally, Alex and Maya invest in assets that generate income **independently of their time**, including:

- Licensing creative content (art, music, templates)
- Software, apps, or plugins
- Patents or inventions

Step-by-Step Process:

1. Create a product or content with enduring value.
2. License it to businesses, platforms, or other creators.
3. Automate royalty tracking and delivery.
4. Reinvest earnings into new content, creating a compounding portfolio.

AI Application:
AI can generate content faster, predict trends, and optimize pricing for digital licenses. Even in emerging

economies, small creators can monetize globally without physical distribution.

$$\$$

Integrating AI Across All Systems

AI is a **force multiplier** for easy money systems:

- **Portfolio Management:** Robo-advisors and AI apps manage investments.

- **Automation:** AI-driven tools automate customer communication, marketing, and workflow.

- **Analytics:** AI predicts trends, identifies profitable niches, and optimizes pricing.

- **Content Creation:** AI generates digital products, educational content, and marketing materials efficiently.

Example in Practice:

Alex and Maya use an AI tool to generate weekly digital content for their online course. AI handles 70% of content creation, while they spend a few hours refining it. The system earns $1,200/month without daily work.

$

Step-by-Step Implementation for Readers

1. **Choose one income stream to start:** Don't overwhelm yourself. Start with a digital product, micro-investment, or rental.

2. **Map the system:** Document steps from creation to delivery and collection.

3. **Identify automation opportunities:** Use AI tools to reduce repetitive work.

4. **Test small:** Invest minimal capital and iterate.

5. **Scale gradually:** As income stabilizes, reinvest into other streams.

6. **Track and optimize:** Use AI analytics or simple dashboards to monitor performance.

By following these steps, anyone can replicate Alex and Maya's approach, even in emerging economies with limited resources.

$

Lifestyle and Psychological Benefits

The results of these systems are profound:

- **Time Freedom:** Income streams continue to work even when they are not actively managing them.

- **Financial Security:** Predictable income reduces anxiety and stress.

- **Compound Growth:** Investments and automated businesses grow steadily over time.

- **Empowerment:** Leveraging AI and systems gives them control over income and future.

The Easy Money Couple lives life on their terms, demonstrating that wealth is **not just accumulation —** **it's freedom, stability, and peace of mind**.

$

Key Takeaways

1. **Systems over effort:** Design income streams that do not require constant attention.

2. **Start small, scale intelligently:** Test each system with low investment before scaling.

3. **Leverage AI wherever possible:** Automation multiplies results, reduces errors, and frees time.

4. **Diversify streams:** Avoid relying on a single source; spread risk across multiple systems.

5. **Document and iterate:** Build knowledge into processes so they can grow independently.

By understanding and applying Alex and Maya's easy money systems, you can create **predictable, compounding, low-stress income streams**, even in challenging economic environments. These strategies form the backbone of your financial foundation, allowing fast money opportunities to be deployed strategically without jeopardizing stability.

Chapter 8
The Strength of Easy Money

While fast money excites with quick wins and rapid growth, easy money impresses through **stability, predictability, and enduring power**. By now, we've seen how Alex and Maya, our Easy Money Couple, build systems that generate income without requiring constant effort. In this chapter, we explore **why these systems are so strong**, how they protect lifestyle and mental health, and how they leverage compounding over time — even in emerging economies — enhanced by AI and technology.

The strength of easy money is subtle but profound. Unlike the adrenaline-driven highs of fast money, easy money provides **freedom, peace, and a foundation that can weather crises**. Understanding this strength is critical for anyone seeking to create wealth that lasts.

$

Predictability: The Core of Easy Money

Predictable income is one of the most underappreciated aspects of wealth. While fast money can spike suddenly, it can just as easily disappear. Easy money, by contrast, is designed to **flow steadily**, providing:

- **Financial confidence:** Knowing that income will arrive without active labor reduces stress.

- **Planning power:** Predictable cash flow allows budgeting for investments, lifestyle, and savings.

- **Flexibility:** With stable income, the couple can take risks elsewhere, such as testing new fast money ideas or investing in growth opportunities.

Example:
Alex and Maya receive a combination of dividend income, automated online sales, and rental revenue each month. Even during economic slowdowns or unexpected events, their systems continue to deliver, creating **resilience that fast money cannot provide alone**.

In emerging economies, this predictability is especially valuable. Markets can be volatile, traditional jobs may be less stable, and inflation may fluctuate sharply. Automated systems, like AI-driven investment platforms or online product sales, can **maintain stability even amid local economic turbulence**.

$

Peace of Mind and Stress Reduction

The psychological benefit of easy money cannot be overstated. With income systems that function independently, Alex and Maya avoid:

- **Financial anxiety:** No need to chase the next deal or scramble for immediate funds.

- **Burnout:** They do not trade their time constantly for money, allowing rest and recovery.

- **Decision fatigue:** Systems and automation handle repetitive tasks, leaving mental energy for strategic choices.

AI Amplification:
Using AI tools such as automated portfolio managers, marketing bots, and virtual assistants, they minimize human error and the stress of managing multiple streams. For example, an AI chatbot handles customer inquiries 24/7 for their online course business, allowing them to focus on strategic growth instead of day-to-day management.

$

Freedom and Lifestyle Flexibility

One of the most tangible strengths of easy money is **control over time**. Alex and Maya are not tied to rigid schedules or labor-intensive work:

- **Choice of work:** They decide what projects to accept, which income streams to expand, and which to pause.

- **Time with family:** Stable systems allow them to plan vacations or personal projects without sacrificing income.

- **Health and well-being:** Flexibility reduces stress-related illness, sleep deprivation, and burnout.

In emerging economies, this flexibility is transformative. Individuals can escape reliance on unstable local employment while building globally competitive online businesses or automated systems, creating **freedom previously reserved for wealthier populations**.

$

Compounding Power: Income That Builds Itself

Perhaps the most underestimated strength of easy money is **compounding**. When systems generate predictable income, that income can be reinvested to create more income, exponentially growing wealth over time.

Key Strategies Alex and Maya Use for Compounding:

1. **Reinvest Dividends:** Dividend-paying stocks are automatically reinvested to buy more shares.

2. **Scale Digital Products:** Profits from one course or ebook fund additional products or marketing campaigns.

3. **Expand Rental Portfolios:** Rental income funds acquisition of additional properties.

4. **Reinvest Freelance Automation:** Earnings from partially automated freelance services fund AI tools and virtual assistants to increase efficiency.

Emerging Economy Example:
Even with modest initial investments, AI tools can accelerate compounding. For instance, a small $100 digital product investment can scale globally using AI-driven marketing and automated delivery, creating a compounding revenue stream that grows faster than traditional methods.

$

Protection of Relationships and Mental Health

Stable income streams protect more than finances — they **protect personal relationships and mental well-being**:

- Couples and families are less likely to argue about money when income is predictable.

- Reduced financial stress allows for healthier parenting, partnership, and personal growth.

- Automation reduces the need for constant attention, allowing mental bandwidth for creative and strategic pursuits.

Alex and Maya use AI to automate mundane tasks, freeing mental space to focus on innovation, relationship quality, and personal fulfillment. This strengthens their bond and allows them to **enjoy the fruits of their labor without constant conflict**.

$

Minimizing Risk Compared to Fast Money

Unlike fast money, easy money systems are **built to withstand shocks**:

- **Diversification:** Multiple streams reduce dependence on any one source.

- **Automation:** Systems continue to operate even during personal emergencies.

- **Predictable cash flow:** Provides a buffer against market downturns or sudden expenses.

AI enhances this resilience. Predictive analytics, automated alerts, and AI-driven risk monitoring help Alex and Maya anticipate problems and adjust their strategies before issues escalate.

$

Combining AI with Easy Money Systems

AI is a **force multiplier** for easy money strategies:

1. **Investment Optimization:** AI analyzes portfolios, predicts trends, and adjusts allocation automatically.

2. **Digital Product Scaling:** AI generates content for online courses, social media, and marketing materials.

3. **Rental & Real Estate Automation:** AI pricing tools optimize rent and occupancy rates.

4. **Business Analytics:** AI dashboards track multiple streams, showing performance metrics in real-time.

In emerging economies, AI tools are a **great equalizer**: anyone with internet access can implement world-class systems, scale rapidly, and compete globally, regardless of initial capital.

$

Lessons and Takeaways

1. **Stability is strength:** Reliable systems provide predictability, freedom, and resilience.

2. **Automation compounds power:** AI and digital tools allow systems to scale without proportional effort.

3. **Lifestyle integration:** Easy money frees time for health, relationships, and personal growth.

4. **Emerging economy advantage:** Automated systems and AI allow small investments to compete globally.

5. **Long-term compounding:** Even modest, predictable streams grow exponentially over years, far surpassing sporadic fast-money wins.

$

Actionable Steps for Readers

1. **Map your current income sources:** Identify which are fast and which can become easy money streams.

2. **Identify one system to automate:** Use AI, software, or outsourcing to reduce manual labor.

3. **Document and repeat:** Create instructions and checklists for each system to scale without daily oversight.

4. **Reinvest profits systematically:** Allocate a portion of every income stream to growth and compounding.

5. **Leverage AI globally:** Use AI tools for investment, marketing, content creation, or business automation to maximize output.

$

Conclusion of Chapter 8

The strength of easy money lies in its **predictability, freedom, and compounding power**. Unlike fast money, which is exciting but volatile, easy money **supports life, reduces stress, and enables strategic growth**. Alex and Maya demonstrate that a well-designed system not only generates income but preserves it, allowing for **peace of mind, lifestyle flexibility, and sustained wealth over decades**.

By integrating AI tools, even those in emerging economies can implement easy money systems, creating **predictable, low-effort, and scalable wealth streams**. These systems provide the foundation upon which fast money can be deployed safely and effectively, ensuring that wealth grows, stabilizes, and endures.

Chapter 9
The Hidden Weaknesses of Easy Money

Easy money may sound like a dream: predictable income, freedom from constant labor, and low stress. But as Alex and Maya discovered, even the most carefully constructed systems have **limitations and hidden risks**. Understanding these weaknesses is essential to avoid complacency, stagnation, or missed opportunities. In this chapter, we'll examine the challenges of easy money, illustrate them with real-world examples, and explore how AI and strategic adjustments can mitigate these risks — even in emerging economies.

While fast money's dangers are obvious — volatility, burnout, and loss — easy money's risks are **subtle but equally consequential**. These weaknesses include slow growth, the need for patience and discipline, susceptibility to boredom or complacency, and potential vulnerability in emergencies.

$

1. Slow Growth Can Be Frustrating

One of the first challenges Alex and Maya faced was the **gradual pace of wealth accumulation**. Unlike fast money, where profits can spike overnight, easy money grows incrementally.

Example:
Their first online course generated $50 in the first week, $100 in the second, and slowly climbed to $1,000 per month over several months. While the trajectory was upward, it lacked the immediate thrill of a high-stakes deal or leveraged investment.

Implications for Readers:

- Patience is not optional. Systems must be trusted to produce results over months or years.

- In emerging economies, slow growth can feel limiting because financial pressures are often immediate. A small initial return may not be sufficient to meet urgent needs.

AI Solution:

- Use AI-driven marketing and analytics to **accelerate early growth**. AI can identify target markets, optimize content, and predict high-conversion opportunities, reducing the slow start phase.

$

2. Patience and Discipline Are Required

Easy money systems depend heavily on **consistent action and ongoing oversight**. Without discipline, these systems can fail quietly:

- Missing reinvestments reduces compounding effects.

- Neglecting maintenance of digital products, rentals, or investment portfolios leads to stagnation.

- Ignoring analytics or system feedback allows small inefficiencies to snowball.

Example:

Alex and Maya once paused updates to their online course for six months. Traffic and sales plateaued because automated systems can only maintain performance; growth requires deliberate optimization.

Practical Tip:

Set recurring reminders or automate checks using AI tools. For example, AI can alert you when engagement drops, investments need rebalancing, or competitors outpace your content.

$

3. Can Feel Boring or Unimpressive Compared to Fast Wins

Humans are naturally drawn to excitement. Easy money lacks immediate drama or thrill, which can lead to **psychological fatigue or disengagement**.

Example:

While watching a friend earn $5,000 in a week from a high-risk crypto trade, Alex and Maya felt a twinge of envy. Their own systems earned $500 per month, steadily but without spectacle.

Implications:

- Without occasional stimulation, it's easy to underestimate the value of slow compounding.

- Boredom can tempt people to abandon systems for faster but riskier ventures.

AI Application:

- Use AI analytics dashboards that visualize growth, compounding, and projections. Seeing tangible metrics over time reinforces motivation.

- AI-generated scenarios can simulate long-term outcomes, helping users appreciate the trajectory of easy money systems.

$

4. Vulnerability During Emergencies

Easy money systems excel in stability but may **fail to address urgent financial crises quickly**:

- Selling digital products, collecting dividends, or relying on rental income may take weeks or months to access during an emergency.

- Automated systems cannot instantly liquidate or pivot without pre-planning.

Example:
When a sudden medical expense arose, Alex and Maya had sufficient emergency savings, but they realized their long-term wealth systems weren't immediately liquid. They had to supplement with a small short-term loan.

Actionable Strategies:

1. **Emergency Fund:** Maintain a cash buffer to cover 3–6 months of expenses.

2. **Flexible Assets:** Include some liquid investments in the portfolio.

3. **AI Alerts:** AI tools can track account balances and project liquidity availability, helping avoid emergencies catching you unprepared.

$

5. Over-Reliance on Systems Can Lead to Complacency

Easy money systems are designed to work independently, but **over-reliance can make investors or entrepreneurs passive**:

- Ignoring market changes can reduce competitiveness.

- Failing to innovate or diversify leads to stagnation.

- Without learning from new technologies or strategies, systems may become outdated.

Example:
A rental property portfolio initially provided excellent cash flow. Over time, urban development patterns

shifted, and some units became less desirable. Because Alex and Maya had relied too heavily on automation without actively analyzing market trends, profits declined temporarily.

AI Mitigation:

- AI can monitor market trends, occupancy rates, and competitor pricing in real-time.

- Automated alerts notify users when a property, investment, or product is underperforming, prompting proactive adjustments.

$

6. Requires Continuous Learning and Adaptation

Even "passive" systems require **ongoing education**:

- Financial literacy is crucial to make informed decisions.

- Technology literacy, particularly AI tools, ensures automation remains efficient.

- Emerging markets may require adaptation to local regulations, currency fluctuations, and digital infrastructure changes.

Example:
Alex and Maya had to learn about AI-driven e-commerce platforms to keep their digital products competitive globally. Failure to adapt would have reduced growth potential.

Practical Steps:

- Dedicate a small portion of time weekly to system review and learning.

- Stay informed about emerging AI tools that could optimize workflows.

- Track global and local market trends to anticipate disruptions.

$

7. Emotional Detachment Can Backfire

Easy money often creates emotional detachment from the process because systems operate independently. While detachment reduces stress, it may also:

- Prevent timely interventions.

- Reduce engagement with clients or customers, impacting reputation.

- Create a false sense of security if systems are not periodically audited.

Solution:

- Implement quarterly system audits, either personally or via AI-assisted analytics.

- Maintain some human oversight in key revenue streams to catch anomalies early.

- Balance automation with strategic engagement.

$

Integrating AI to Offset Weaknesses

AI is not a cure-all, but it mitigates many easy money weaknesses:

1. **Acceleration:** AI marketing and analytics reduce slow growth periods.

2. **Discipline Enforcement:** AI scheduling and alert systems enforce consistent action.

3. **Visualization:** AI dashboards combat boredom by illustrating long-term growth.

4. **Emergency Preparedness:** AI tracks liquidity and warns of shortfalls.

5. **Adaptation:** AI monitors market shifts and suggests changes to maintain system performance.

Emerging Economy Advantage:
Even small-scale operators in developing markets can use AI to offset traditional weaknesses of easy money: speed

up growth, manage complexity, and reduce risk without large teams or capital.

$

Key Takeaways

1. Easy money is powerful, but slow growth requires **patience and consistent effort**.

2. Automated systems must be **monitored and optimized** to avoid stagnation.

3. Predictability can feel boring, so tracking progress visually helps maintain motivation.

4. Emergency funds and liquid assets are essential to cover fast financial shocks.

5. AI tools can mitigate nearly every weakness, but human oversight remains critical.

6. Continuous learning ensures systems remain relevant, effective, and profitable.

$

Actionable Steps for Readers

1. Conduct a **system audit** of all passive or automated income streams. Identify gaps, bottlenecks, or vulnerabilities.

2. Establish or verify an **emergency fund** separate from long-term investments.

3. Introduce **AI monitoring and analytics tools** for each income stream.

4. Commit to a **quarterly review schedule**, assessing performance, growth, and market shifts.

5. Plan for **system updates** or reinvestment to maintain long-term growth and relevance.

$

Conclusion of Chapter 9

Easy money offers remarkable benefits — predictability, peace, and compounding growth — but it is **not without hidden challenges**. Slow growth, patience demands, potential boredom, emergencies, and over-reliance on automation are risks that, if ignored, can undermine success.

Alex and Maya demonstrate that **awareness, discipline, and AI-assisted oversight** can neutralize most weaknesses, making easy money a powerful foundation for lasting wealth. By understanding these challenges and proactively addressing them, readers can maximize the strengths of easy money while avoiding the subtle traps that could erode stability.

Chapter 10
Easy Money Lessons You Can Use

While Chapters 6–9 explored the mindset, systems, strengths, and weaknesses of easy money, this chapter focuses on **practical lessons and step-by-step strategies you can implement immediately**. The Easy Money Couple — Alex and Maya — demonstrates that slow, predictable wealth is not passive because it requires **intentional design, consistency, and strategic automation**.

This chapter provides actionable methods to create and scale income streams, leveraging **AI tools, automation platforms, and global opportunities**, including strategies specifically adaptable for emerging economies. By following these lessons, you can replicate the principles of easy money without needing large capital or high-risk ventures.

$

Lesson 1: Document Every System

Why it matters:
A system is only as strong as its instructions. Documenting each step ensures **repeatability, scalability, and resilience**.

Step-by-Step Implementation:

1. Choose an income stream (digital product, investment, rental, or automated service).

2. Break it into actionable steps: creation, delivery, marketing, management, reinvestment.

3. Write or record each step in a process guide. Include screenshots, templates, or AI-generated instructions.

4. Assign roles if you outsource: the clearer the instructions, the easier for virtual assistants or AI tools to follow.

Example:
Alex and Maya documented the process of creating an online course: idea selection, content creation, AI content

assistance, marketing automation, and customer service flow. This guide allowed them to replicate the process for multiple courses with minimal effort.

AI Tip:
Use AI platforms like Notion AI or ChatGPT to automatically generate step-by-step SOPs for your systems. In emerging markets, this ensures even small teams or solo operators can scale globally.

$

2: Automate as Much as Possible

Automation transforms a good system into an **easy money system**. It reduces errors, saves time, and allows income streams to run independently.

Step-by-Step Implementation:

1. Identify repetitive tasks: content scheduling, client communication, bookkeeping.

2. Research AI and automation tools for each task:

- o AI chatbots for customer support (e.g., ChatGPT, ManyChat).

- o Social media scheduling (e.g., Buffer, Hootsuite).

- o Automated investment and portfolio management (e.g., Robo-advisors).

3. Set up triggers and workflows: AI handles tasks when conditions are met.

4. Monitor performance weekly, adjusting rules or AI prompts as needed.

Example:
Alex and Maya use an AI chatbot to handle online course inquiries, freeing them from daily emails. The bot provides instant responses, upsells products, and escalates complex issues.

Emerging Market Application:
Even in regions with limited internet infrastructure, AI

chatbots can manage WhatsApp, Messenger, or Telegram inquiries, reducing the need for large teams.

$

Lesson 3: Start Small, Scale Slowly

Easy money relies on **incremental growth**. Starting small minimizes risk while allowing learning and refinement.

Step-by-Step Implementation:

1. Launch a single income stream with minimal investment.

2. Test assumptions: market demand, pricing, delivery process.

3. Collect data and refine systems.

4. Once proven, reinvest profits to scale the stream or replicate it with new systems.

Example:
Alex and Maya initially sold a $5 ebook. After observing demand, they expanded to $50 online courses and

memberships. The initial small investment allowed them to iterate before scaling.

AI Tip:
Use AI analytics tools to predict demand, optimize pricing, and identify trends. This accelerates decision-making and reduces trial-and-error costs.

$

Lesson 4: Leverage Multiple Income Streams

Relying on one stream is risky. Alex and Maya diversify across:

- Investments (dividends, REITs, bonds)

- Digital products (courses, templates, guides)

- Rental or real estate income

- Automated service or freelance businesses

- Licensing or intellectual property

Step-by-Step Implementation:

1. List potential streams you can realistically manage.

2. Allocate time and resources proportionally to test each.

3. Track performance via dashboards or AI analytics.

4. Gradually scale the most profitable and consistent streams.

Emerging Market Example:
Digital products can be sold internationally, while AI-assisted freelance services reach clients globally. Small investments in local real estate or micro-rentals add additional stability.

$

Lesson 5: Reinvest for Compounding Growth

Easy money grows exponentially when profits are reinvested. Alex and Maya allocate **a portion of every stream** to:

- Scaling existing systems

- Funding new digital products

- Investing in automated tools or AI enhancements

Step-by-Step Implementation:

1. Define reinvestment percentages for each income stream.

2. Automate reinvestment where possible (e.g., dividends reinvested, digital product revenue funneled into marketing).

3. Monitor returns quarterly to optimize allocation.

AI Tip:
Use AI financial planning tools to simulate reinvestment outcomes and maximize compounding.

$

Lesson 6: Maintain Liquidity and Emergency Funds

Even predictable income requires **financial buffers** to handle emergencies:

1. Maintain a minimum of 3–6 months of expenses in liquid accounts.

2. Allocate funds for unexpected repairs, sudden business expenses, or market shocks.

3. Use AI to monitor cash flow and alert you if liquidity falls below thresholds.

Example:
Alex and Maya's rental income may be delayed occasionally. By maintaining a small emergency fund, they avoid stress and can reinvest smoothly without interrupting growth.

$

Lesson 7: Continuous Optimization and Learning

Automation does not mean "set it and forget it." Systems must evolve:

- Review metrics monthly or quarterly.

- Test improvements in small iterations.

- Stay updated on AI tools, emerging platforms, and global market shifts.

Example:
Alex and Maya discovered a new AI video platform that improved their digital course creation speed by 50%. Integrating this tool accelerated revenue without increasing manual effort.

Emerging Market Application:
AI allows small operators to compete globally with minimal overhead. Even low-resource environments can implement best practices in automated business and passive income.

$

Lesson 8: Prioritize Balance and Lifestyle

Finally, easy money should serve life, not consume it:

- Schedule personal and family time.

- Align income streams with values and long-term goals.

- Avoid the trap of adding streams unnecessarily, which increases complexity without meaningful benefit.

Example:
Alex and Maya carefully chose which digital products to scale and which rental properties to acquire. They prioritized streams that aligned with their lifestyle, allowing **time freedom and peace of mind**.

$

Actionable Checklist for Readers

1. Document all income systems and processes.

2. Automate repetitive tasks using AI and software tools.

3. Start one income stream with minimal investment.

4. Test, measure, and refine before scaling.

5. Diversify streams to reduce risk.

6. Reinvest profits to compound growth.

7. Maintain liquidity and emergency funds.

8. Optimize systems continuously using analytics and AI.

9. Align streams with lifestyle and long-term goals.

By following this checklist, you can replicate Alex and Maya's easy money success while minimizing risks, leveraging technology, and building wealth predictably.

$

Conclusion of Chapter 10

Easy money is a **strategy of discipline, systems, and compounding growth**, enhanced by AI and automation. The lessons outlined here provide a **step-by-step blueprint** for anyone seeking stable, scalable income streams. Whether in a developed market or an emerging economy, these strategies enable individuals to **create predictable wealth, free up time, and build a**

foundation that supports fast money opportunities safely.

By implementing these systems, you can **enjoy financial stability, lifestyle flexibility, and long-term wealth growth**, setting the stage for the next chapters where we compare fast and easy money approaches and integrate them into a holistic wealth-building plan.

PART III:

CROSSROAD

WHAT BOTH PATHS GET
RIGHT & WRONG

Chapter 11
When Fast Money Meets Easy Money

Up to this point, we've examined two contrasting approaches to wealth creation. Fast money offers adrenaline, quick wins, and high-stakes opportunities, while easy money provides stability, predictability, and compounding growth. Alex and Maya, the Easy Money Couple, exemplify the power of systems, automation, and patience, whereas the Fast Money Couple — Jordan and Leila — illustrate the allure and volatility of rapid financial gain.

In this chapter, we explore **how these two approaches intersect, complement, and sometimes conflict**. Understanding the interplay between fast and easy money is essential for building a holistic financial strategy that maximizes opportunity while minimizing risk. We also present **practical steps to integrate both approaches**, even in emerging economies, leveraging AI and technology to optimize outcomes.

$

Side-by-Side Comparison: Wins and Losses

Let's examine the key outcomes of each couple's approach:

Aspect	Fast Money (Jordan & Leila)	Easy Money (Alex & Maya)
Income Trajectory	Spikes rapidly but volatile	Slow, steady, and compounding
Stress Levels	High due to risk and volatility	Low, predictable, and manageable
Lifestyle Impact	Often chaotic; burnouts common	Flexible and balanced
Relationship Health	Strained due to financial pressure	Strengthened due to predictability

Aspect	Fast Money (Jordan & Leila)	Easy Money (Alex & Maya)
Wealth Longevity	Often short-lived without reinvestment	Long-term, scalable, and resilient
Opportunities for AI Integration	AI can optimize trades, detect trends, and reduce risk	AI automates systems, scaling without constant labor
Best Use Case	Funding large opportunities or rapid growth	Building foundational wealth and compounding income

Observation:

Fast money acts as a **fuel** — providing energy and capital to seize opportunities. Easy money acts as a **foundation**, ensuring that wealth persists, grows, and supports lifestyle stability. Individually, each approach has strengths and weaknesses. Together, they can create **synergistic wealth strategies**.

$

How Each Path Built or Destroyed Opportunity

Fast Money Highlights

- **Wins:** Jordan and Leila leveraged high-risk investments, flipping, and leveraged trades to generate rapid gains. They capitalized on market trends, personal networks, and timing to grow their wealth quickly.

- **Losses:** Mismanaged deals, impulsive decisions, and lack of systems often led to setbacks. Emotional reactions amplified losses, and relationships suffered from financial volatility.

Easy Money Highlights

- **Wins:** Alex and Maya consistently built income systems that generated reliable cash flow. Investments, rentals, and digital products provided steady growth, with compounding effects over time. Their lifestyle and relationships remained intact.

- **Losses:** Growth was slow, and emergency situations revealed vulnerabilities in liquidity. Without integrating some fast money opportunities, certain high-return possibilities were missed.

Lesson:

While fast money creates opportunity, it requires discipline, oversight, and systems to avoid collapse. Easy money builds resilience and long-term wealth, but may not seize high-return opportunities quickly. **The key is strategic integration.**

$$\$$

Where Strategies Overlap

Despite differences, there are natural points of overlap between fast and easy money:

1. **Reinvestment:** Both approaches recognize that profits should be reinvested. Fast money can fund new systems; easy money can fund new ventures.

2. **Automation:** Fast money gains efficiency when AI tools assist decision-making and trading. Easy money thrives on automation to scale and reduce labor.

3. **Skill Transfer:** Skills acquired from fast-money ventures — market analysis, negotiation, trend recognition — can enhance easy money systems.

4. **Data-Driven Decisions:** Both approaches benefit from analytics. AI tools can detect patterns, optimize processes, and improve outcomes across both streams.

Example:
Alex and Maya used profits from a fast-money crypto venture to fund AI tools that automated their digital

product business. This accelerated growth and reduced manual work, combining the speed of fast money with the stability of easy money.

$

- **Where Strategies Contradict Each Other**

Integration requires caution because **conflicting approaches can undermine each other**:

- **Risk Appetite:** Fast money thrives on risk-taking; easy money prioritizes risk mitigation.

- **Time Horizon:** Fast money focuses on immediate gains; easy money focuses on decades-long compounding.

- **Emotional Management:** Fast money can induce stress and reactive decisions, which may disrupt steady systems.

Solution:

- Treat fast money as a **capital generation tool** to fund easy money systems.

- Set clear boundaries: allocate only a portion of wealth or time to high-risk ventures.

- Maintain automated, resilient easy money systems to buffer against fast money volatility.

$

Integrating Fast and Easy Money: The Holistic Model

The goal is to create a **balanced strategy**:

1. **50/30/20 Allocation:**

   o 50% of fast money profits → reinvest into easy money systems (foundation).

- 30% → reinvest in additional fast money ventures (growth).

- 20% → lifestyle or debt reduction (security).

2. **AI-Enhanced Integration:**

   - AI investment tools can manage both fast trades and stable portfolios simultaneously.

   - Automation ensures easy money systems are not disrupted by fast money volatility.

3. **Scenario Planning:**

   - Map out multiple financial scenarios to determine how much capital to allocate to each approach.

   - AI simulations can model outcomes under different risk profiles and market conditions.

$

Practical Steps for Readers

1. **Map Your Income Streams:** Identify fast vs. easy money sources.

2. **Allocate Wisely:** Decide how much capital, time, and effort to assign to each approach.

3. **Automate Systems:** Use AI tools to scale easy money while monitoring fast-money risks.

4. **Set Rules:** Clearly define thresholds for exiting high-risk ventures to protect foundation wealth.

5. **Track Metrics:** Dashboards for both types of income ensure visibility and informed decisions.

6. **Reinvest Strategically:** Fast money fuels opportunities; easy money compounds wealth.

$

Emerging Economy Applications

Integration is especially powerful in emerging economies:

- **Fast Money:** Micro-investments, trading small-scale commodities, or flipping goods online can generate rapid returns.

- **Easy Money:** AI-powered digital businesses, micro-rentals, and automated online services create stability.

- **Synergy:** Fast money can fund AI tools that automate local online businesses, enabling small investors to scale globally.

Example:

A small e-commerce store in Southeast Asia can be funded with fast money from local flips or short-term trades. AI tools handle inventory, customer queries, and marketing, while profits compound via digital product creation or micro-investments.

$

Lessons Learned from Both Couples

1. **Fast Money Provides Opportunity; Easy Money Preserves It:** Capital is only valuable if it is managed wisely.

2. **Integration is Key:** One without the other creates imbalance — either short-term thrill with no sustainability or slow growth with missed opportunities.

3. **AI and Automation Are Force Multipliers:** Both streams benefit from efficiency, scalability, and predictive analytics.

4. **Boundaries Protect Systems:** Fast-money risks must be compartmentalized to avoid destabilizing easy money foundations.

$

Key Takeaways

- Treat fast money as fuel for long-term growth.

- Ensure easy money systems are robust before taking high-risk opportunities.

- Leverage AI to manage complexity, automate tasks, and optimize performance.

- Maintain discipline, documentation, and reinvestment practices for maximum compounding.

- Use emerging economy opportunities strategically, balancing immediate gains with sustainable growth.

$

Actionable Steps

1. **Audit your current wealth streams**: Identify fast vs. easy money.

2. **Allocate profits strategically** using the 50/30/20 framework.

3. **Integrate AI tools** to optimize both fast and easy money systems.

4. **Document processes** for easy money systems to withstand volatility.

5. **Simulate scenarios** to understand the impact of fast-money gains or losses on foundation systems.

6. **Reinvest intelligently**, using fast-money profits to accelerate easy-money growth.

$

Conclusion of Chapter 11

When fast money meets easy money, wealth creation becomes **both powerful and sustainable**. Fast money provides speed, capital, and opportunity; easy money provides stability, compounding growth, and lifestyle freedom. By learning from both couples —

Jordan and Leila for fast money, Alex and Maya for easy money — and leveraging AI tools to integrate their strategies, readers can achieve **balanced, resilient, and scalable financial success**, even in emerging economies.

Chapter 12
Do The Real Truth About Wealth Shadow

Wealth is not simply the sum of money in a bank account or the number of assets owned. True, sustainable wealth combines **capital, systems, strategy, and foresight**. In Chapters 1–11, we've examined the dynamics of fast money, easy money, and the interaction between the two. This chapter distills the **real truth about wealth**: that it requires both **speed and stability, risk and structure, fuel and foundation**.

Alex and Maya, the Easy Money Couple, and Jordan and Leila, the Fast Money Couple, illustrate that neither approach is sufficient alone. The key to enduring prosperity lies in **strategic integration**, leveraging both fast and easy money streams in a unified framework, enhanced by AI, automation, and global opportunities — even in emerging economies.

$

Why Sustainable Wealth Requires Both Fast and Easy Money

Wealth has two essential dimensions:

1. **Liquidity and Capital Acceleration (Fast Money):**
   Fast money provides **rapid inflows of capital**, enabling investment in new opportunities, business expansion, and high-return ventures. Without it, slow systems may not reach critical mass quickly enough to compete or capitalize on emerging trends.

2. **Foundation and Stability (Easy Money):**
   Easy money creates **predictable, compounding, and resilient income streams**. It ensures that wealth survives market fluctuations, economic crises, and personal setbacks. Without this foundation, even large fast-money gains can dissipate quickly.

Observation:
Wealth that ignores either component is incomplete. Fast money without systems collapses under risk. Easy money without capital injection grows slowly and may miss opportunities. Integrating both produces **financial resilience, growth, and freedom**.

$

Fast Money = Fuel

Think of fast money as the **engine fuel of wealth**:

- It powers growth, enabling investments, acquisitions, and high-return ventures.

- It provides emergency liquidity or opportunities that require immediate capital.

- It excites, motivating continued effort and learning.

Examples of Fast Money as Fuel:

- Flipping undervalued properties, then reinvesting gains into automated rentals.

- Short-term stock trades or cryptocurrency investments funding AI-driven digital businesses.

- Side hustles generating capital for long-term passive income platforms.

Emerging Economy Application:
Even in resource-constrained environments, small fast-money opportunities — like online arbitrage, freelance projects, or local product flips — can provide fuel to fund automated digital systems or micro-investments.

$

Easy Money = Foundation

Easy money serves as the **structural support**:

- Provides consistent income to cover living costs, reduce stress, and fund reinvestment.

- Enables compounding, scaling, and automation without continuous attention.

- Protects wealth from volatility and risk inherent in fast-money ventures.

Examples of Easy Money Foundations:

- Dividend portfolios reinvesting profits over decades.

- Automated digital product systems generating global sales.

- Rental income secured through property management and AI-assisted optimization.

Emerging Economy Application:
Small-scale online businesses, micro-rentals, and AI-managed investment portfolios allow individuals to build foundational wealth, even with limited initial capital.

$

The Two-Bucket Wealth Model

To integrate fast and easy money effectively, we introduce the **Two-Bucket Wealth Model**:

1. **Bucket 1 – Fast Money (Fuel):**

   o Allocated for high-growth opportunities.

   o Risk-tolerant, liquid, and designed for acceleration.

   o Example allocation: 30–50% of capital.

2. **Bucket 2 – Easy Money (Foundation):**

   o Allocated for predictable, compounding, and automated income streams.

   o Low-risk, stable, and designed for long-term accumulation.

      o Example allocation: 50–70% of capital.

How it works:

- Fast money generates capital spikes that feed into easy money systems.

- Easy money preserves and compounds capital, ensuring that wealth persists even if fast-money ventures fail.

- Over time, the two buckets create a **self-reinforcing cycle of wealth growth**.

$$\$$$

AI as a Force Multiplier in the Two-Bucket Model

AI tools enhance both buckets:

- **Fast Money:**

      o AI-driven analytics identify high-return opportunities.

- o Predictive modeling minimizes risk and maximizes returns.

- o Automation ensures trades or projects are executed with precision and speed.

- **Easy Money:**

  - o AI automates recurring revenue streams, from digital products to rental management.

  - o Analytics dashboards track performance and alert to inefficiencies.

  - o AI tools simulate compounding scenarios to guide reinvestment and scaling.

Emerging Economy Application:
AI democratizes wealth-building: even with minimal capital, individuals can identify opportunities, automate systems, and optimize income streams globally.

$

Lessons from Both Couples

By comparing the two couples, we derive key lessons:

1. **Leverage Fast Money Responsibly:** Use quick gains to fund systems, not to fund lifestyle inflation alone.

2. **Prioritize Easy Money Systems:** They protect wealth and provide stability to handle fast-money volatility.

3. **Integrate, Don't Isolate:** Fast and easy money should interact in a structured plan.

4. **Use Technology:** AI, automation, and analytics tools amplify the efficiency and security of both approaches.

5. **Plan for Emergencies:** Liquidity from fast-money channels and predictability from easy-money systems create resilience against unexpected shocks.

$

Practical Steps to Apply the Two-Bucket Model

1. **Assess Current Resources:** Identify all existing fast and easy money streams.

2. **Allocate Capital:** Decide what portion of your funds goes into each bucket (e.g., 50% easy, 30% fast, 20% lifestyle/emergencies).

3. **Automate Easy Money Systems:** Deploy AI-driven automation, dashboards, and virtual assistants to reduce manual effort.

4. **Select Fast Money Opportunities:** Identify high-return ventures aligned with your risk tolerance. Use AI tools to analyze markets and predict performance.

5. **Reinvest Strategically:** Fast-money profits should feed easy-

money systems to accelerate compounding.

6. **Monitor and Adjust:** Quarterly reviews using AI dashboards ensure both buckets remain optimized and balanced.

$

Case Study: Applying the Model in an Emerging Economy

Scenario:

- A small entrepreneur in Southeast Asia starts with $200 in savings.

- **Fast Money Bucket:** Invests $50 in local online arbitrage and freelance projects. Gains $150 in one month.

- **Easy Money Bucket:** Invests $100 in AI-assisted digital products and small online courses. Generates $20/month passive income.

- **Integration:** Fast money profits fund more digital products, expanding the passive income foundation.

Outcome:

- Within six months, passive income grows to $150/month, and fast-money ventures provide capital for further scaling.

- The entrepreneur now has a **balanced system**: predictable income and scalable opportunity.

$

Key Takeaways

1. **True wealth requires balance:** Fuel and foundation work together to maximize growth and stability.

2. **Fast money alone is risky; easy money alone is slow:** Integration ensures speed, security, and sustainability.

3. **AI amplifies both approaches:** Predictive analytics, automation, and decision-support systems enhance results.

4. **Emerging economies benefit disproportionately:** Automation and AI enable global competition with minimal capital.

5. **Systematic reinvestment compounds wealth:** Fast-money gains accelerate easy-money growth for long-term financial security.

$

Actionable Checklist

1. Identify all fast and easy money streams.

2. Allocate capital using the Two-Bucket Wealth Model.

3. Automate easy money systems with AI tools.

4. Select high-return, risk-aligned fast money opportunities.

5. Reinvest fast-money profits into easy-money foundations.

6. Track performance and optimize quarterly using dashboards and analytics.

7. Maintain liquidity for emergencies.

8. Continuously learn and adapt to new AI tools and market opportunities.

$

Conclusion of Chapter 12

The real truth about wealth is that it is **both fast and slow, aggressive and stable, exciting and predictable**. Fast money provides the fuel to seize opportunities and accelerate growth. Easy money provides the foundation to preserve, compound, and secure that wealth. By implementing the Two-Bucket Wealth Model and leveraging AI, automation, and strategic reinvestment, anyone — regardless of location or initial capital — can **build sustainable, scalable, and resilient wealth**.

Wealth is not a sprint or a gamble; it is a **systematic process**, guided by strategy, technology, and disciplined execution. With the lessons from both couples, readers can now take confident steps toward **integrating speed and stability into their financial journey**.

PART IV

THE BLUEPRINT

HOW THE READER CAN WIN

Chapter 13
Building Your Fast Money Engine

Fast money is the **engine of wealth creation**. It provides speed, opportunity, and capital necessary to scale wealth quickly. But without structure, discipline, and clear systems, fast money can be fleeting, leaving stress, losses, and burnout in its wake.

In this chapter, we explore how to **design, build, and operate a fast-money engine**, drawing lessons from Jordan and Leila, the Fast Money Couple, and integrating **AI, automation, and proven strategies** that anyone can apply — even in emerging economies.

$

Step 1: Choose the Right Fast-Money Vehicle

Not all fast-money opportunities are created equal. Choosing the right vehicle depends on **risk tolerance, capital, skills, and market conditions**.

Categories of Fast Money Vehicles:

1. Flipping and Arbitrage:

- Buying undervalued assets (real estate, products, digital assets) and selling for a profit.

- Requires market knowledge, negotiation skills, and timing.

- Example: Flipping smartphones or second-hand furniture online.

2. High-Risk Investments:

- Short-term stock trades, options, cryptocurrencies, or commodities.

- Requires market analysis, risk management, and monitoring tools.

- AI Tip: Use predictive trading platforms or algorithmic trading bots to identify high-probability opportunities.

3. **Side Hustles and Freelancing:**

- Skills-based services (design, copywriting, consulting) monetized quickly.

- AI Tip: Use AI tools to enhance productivity, generate proposals, and automate client communication.

4. **Short-Term Ventures:**

- Pop-up businesses, seasonal products, event-based services.

- Requires low setup time and rapid execution.

- Example: Selling trending products on e-commerce platforms.

Practical Exercise:
List 5 potential fast-money vehicles aligned with your skills, capital, and risk tolerance. Rank them by feasibility, ROI potential, and scalability.

$

Step 2: Test Ideas Quickly

Fast money thrives on **speed and iteration**. The goal is to test ideas rapidly, learn, and pivot before committing significant resources.

Step-by-Step Implementation:

1. **Small Initial Investment:** Test with minimal funds to limit losses.

2. **Short Timelines:** Set deadlines for proof-of-concept or ROI evaluation.

3. **Data Collection:** Track every metric — profit, cost, time investment, market response.

4. **Iterate or Pivot:** Use results to refine the idea or switch to a new opportunity.

Example:
Jordan invested $200 in a local trending product. After a week, he analyzed sales, demand, and costs. The initial

test showed strong demand, prompting a $1,000 reinvestment.

AI Integration:

- AI analytics platforms can track sales, social media trends, and competitor behavior.

- Predictive modeling helps anticipate demand and optimize product pricing.

$

Step 3: Build Repeatable Systems

Fast money is not luck — it's **engineered through systems**. Repetition and scalability distinguish sustainable fast-money earners from those who fail.

Step-by-Step Implementation:

1. **Document Every Step:** Record sourcing, marketing, sales, and delivery processes.

2. **Automate Where Possible:** Use AI or software tools for repetitive tasks.

3. **Outsource:** Delegate low-value tasks to virtual assistants or contractors.

4. **Monitor Metrics:** Track ROI, time invested, and scalability potential.

Example:

Jordan created a system for flipping electronics: sourcing via online marketplaces, pricing using AI trend analysis, and outsourcing delivery to local couriers. The system allowed him to scale from 1–2 sales per week to 50–100 sales per week.

$

Step 4: Scale Strategically

Scaling is the difference between **temporary wins and sustained fast-money income**. Scaling without systems leads to chaos and burnout.

Step-by-Step Implementation:

1. **Reinvest Profits:** Allocate a portion of gains back into expanding inventory, marketing, or automation.

2. **Increase Capacity Gradually:** Don't double investments blindly; scale in measured increments.

3. **Optimize Operations:** Identify bottlenecks and improve efficiency using AI tools.

4. **Expand Market Reach:** Use digital platforms, partnerships, or AI-driven advertising.

AI Tip:
- Automated ad targeting, sales funnels, and inventory management allow rapid scaling without proportionally increasing manual labor.

$

Step 5: Know When to Keep Going and When to Quit

Not all fast-money ventures succeed. The key is **disciplined exit strategies**.

Step-by-Step Implementation:

1. **Set Profit and Loss Thresholds:** Decide in advance how much loss is acceptable and what profit triggers scaling.

2. **Monitor Market Signals:** Use AI tools to track market changes, trends, or competitor actions.

3. **Document Lessons Learned:** Every failure teaches critical insights for future ventures.

4. **Reallocate Resources:** Move capital from failing ventures to better-performing opportunities.

Example:

Jordan had a high-risk crypto trade that underperformed expectations. By using AI alerts and pre-set thresholds, he exited at a minor loss, preserving capital for a better opportunity.

$

Step 6: Protect Yourself Legally and Financially

Fast money comes with **legal and financial risks**. Preparation ensures that profits aren't lost to avoidable mistakes.

Step-by-Step Implementation:

1. **Separate Personal and Business Accounts:** Track profits and taxes clearly.

2. **Contracts and Agreements:** Use legal documents for partnerships, clients, or vendors.

3. **Insurance:** Consider coverage for high-value assets or business operations.

4. **Tax Compliance:** Maintain records and work with professionals to avoid penalties.

AI Tip:
AI accounting software and document automation can

manage compliance, track profits, and generate contracts efficiently.

$

Step 7: Integrate Fast Money With Easy Money

Fast money should **feed and strengthen easy money systems**, creating compounding wealth.

Practical Implementation:

1. Allocate a portion of profits to easy money foundations: automated digital products, rental income, dividend portfolios.

2. Use fast-money profits to fund AI tools that enhance easy money scalability.

3. Balance risk exposure: don't let fast-money losses destabilize your easy-money foundation.

Example:
Jordan reinvested 50% of profits from a short-term flip into an AI-driven online course platform. The platform

generated consistent passive income, stabilizing his financial growth.

$

Step 8: Continuous Learning and Optimization

Fast money is **dynamic**, requiring ongoing adaptation:

- Monitor trends, markets, and emerging AI tools.

- Optimize processes based on performance data.

- Learn from both successes and failures.

Emerging Economy Application:
AI allows entrepreneurs in low-capital environments to **predict trends, scale with minimal resources, and reduce trial-and-error**, effectively leveling the playing field globally.

$

Actionable Checklist for Building Your Fast Money Engine

1. Identify high-return, low-capital fast-money opportunities.

2. Test ideas with small investments and short timelines.

3. Document all processes and create repeatable systems.

4. Automate tasks using AI and software tools.

5. Scale gradually and strategically.

6. Set clear exit strategies and monitor market signals.

7. Protect your assets legally and financially.

8. Reinvest profits to enhance easy-money foundations.

9. Continuously optimize systems and leverage AI for predictive insights.

$

Conclusion of Chapter 13

A fast-money engine is not a gamble — it is a **structured, disciplined system** that generates rapid capital and opportunities. When designed properly, it fuels your wealth-building journey without compromising your long-term stability. By combining **strategic vehicle selection, rapid testing, scalable systems, AI integration, and disciplined exits**, readers can create a fast-money engine that powers both immediate gains and long-term prosperity.

In the next chapter, we will examine **how to set up your easy-money foundation**, showing step-by-step methods to transform fast-money gains into **predictable, compounding, long-term wealth**.

Chapter 14
Setting Up Your Easy Money Foundation

If fast money is the engine that powers wealth, easy money is the **foundation that holds it up**. Without a strong foundation, gains from high-speed ventures can evaporate quickly, leaving stress, instability, and missed opportunities.

Alex and Maya, the Easy Money Couple, demonstrate that **predictable, automated, and compounding income systems** provide long-term stability, lifestyle freedom, and resilience against market volatility. In this chapter, we will break down **step-by-step methods to create your easy money foundation**, integrating AI, automation, and global opportunities — even in emerging economies.

$

Step 1: Automate Savings and Income

The first step in building easy money is **consistent, automated cash flow**. Automation ensures that wealth grows without requiring constant attention.

Step-by-Step Implementation:

1. **Automate Savings:**

   - Set up recurring transfers to a dedicated savings or investment account.

   - Example: Transfer 20–30% of all income automatically each month.

2. **Automate Income Streams:**

   - Use AI and automation tools to manage recurring revenue sources:

     - Digital products (e-books, courses, templates).

- Affiliate marketing programs.

- Rental or subscription services.

3. **Automate Expense Tracking:**

   o Use apps like Mint, QuickBooks, or AI-driven budgeting tools to track cash flow and identify savings opportunities.

Emerging Economy Application:
Even with limited banking infrastructure, digital wallets, mobile money services, and AI-assisted bookkeeping apps allow automation for both income and savings, ensuring predictability.

$

Step 2: Build Predictable, Low-Effort Income Streams

Easy money relies on systems that generate revenue **without daily effort**. The goal is to create income that works while you sleep.

Categories of Easy Money Income:

1. **Digital Products:**

   o Courses, templates, guides, and e-books.

   o AI tools can assist with content creation, editing, and marketing.

   o Example: Alex and Maya created an online course once, which sold globally for years with automated marketing.

2. **Rental Income:**

   o Residential or commercial rentals, or co-living arrangements.

   o AI can optimize pricing, manage bookings, and handle tenant communication.

3. **Dividend or Interest Investments:**

- o Stocks, ETFs, REITs, and bonds.

- o AI-powered robo-advisors manage portfolios, reinvest dividends, and optimize returns.

4. **Automated Online Services:**

- o E-commerce, print-on-demand, SaaS tools.

- o AI chatbots, scheduling, and marketing automation reduce labor.

Practical Exercise:

Select two low-effort income streams you can implement this year. Document the system and identify areas for AI automation.

$

Step 3: Build Long-Term Compounding Wealth

Compounding is the **core principle of easy money**. By reinvesting income and profits, wealth grows exponentially over time.

Step-by-Step Implementation:

1. Allocate a fixed percentage of income streams to reinvestment.

2. Choose investment vehicles with compounding potential:

   o Dividend-paying stocks, mutual funds, ETFs.

   o Automated digital product sales platforms.

3. Use AI tools to simulate compounding scenarios, projecting growth over 1, 5, 10, and 20 years.

4. Avoid unnecessary withdrawals that disrupt compounding.

Example:
Alex reinvested profits from her first digital course into creating three additional courses. Within two years, automated sales generated a compounding revenue stream that surpassed her initial investments.

$

Step 4: Leverage Time, Technology, and Outsourcing

Easy money is built on **leverage** — not working harder, but smarter.

Step-by-Step Implementation:

1. **Time Leverage:**
   - Focus on creating systems once that produce revenue repeatedly.
   - Delegate repetitive tasks.

2. **Technology Leverage:**
   - Use AI to automate tasks like customer support, content creation, and marketing.

- o Implement software to manage portfolios, track metrics, and optimize revenue streams.

3. **Outsourcing Leverage:**

- o Hire virtual assistants or freelancers to handle operational tasks.

- o Use platforms like Fiverr, Upwork, or regional equivalents.

Emerging Economy Application:
Global platforms and AI allow small teams or solo entrepreneurs to manage digital and physical assets efficiently, reducing the need for large local infrastructure.

$

Step 5: Monitor and Optimize Your Systems

Automation does not mean "set it and forget it." Continuous monitoring ensures that systems remain efficient, profitable, and aligned with long-term goals.

Step-by-Step Implementation:

1. Track key performance metrics: revenue, profit margins, customer acquisition cost, and growth rate.

2. Use AI dashboards to detect inefficiencies or anomalies in real time.

3. Test small changes systematically to improve performance.

4. Document improvements to refine systems and scale without reinventing the wheel.

Example:

Maya used an AI analytics dashboard to track her online course performance. She identified underperforming marketing channels and adjusted automatically, increasing revenue without additional manual effort.

$

Step 6: Protect Your Foundation

Even low-risk systems require **legal, financial, and operational safeguards**.

Step-by-Step Implementation:

1. **Legal Protections:**

   o Incorporate businesses, register intellectual property, and use contracts for outsourcing.

2. **Financial Protections:**

   o Separate personal and business accounts.

   o Maintain emergency funds and insurance.

3. **Operational Protections:**

   o Back up digital products, data, and records.

o Use AI to monitor system health, detect anomalies, and automate alerts.

Emerging Economy Application:
Even in less developed legal environments, structured contracts, digital agreements, and virtual banking can safeguard assets and systems.

$$\$$

Step 7: Scale Your Easy Money Foundation

Once systems are reliable, scaling increases compounding returns:

1. Reinvest a portion of profits into new systems or additional units of existing streams.

2. Use AI to identify market trends, customer behavior, and growth opportunities.

3. Expand reach globally to maximize revenue potential.

Example:

Alex and Maya reinvested their rental profits into a digital course platform with global marketing. AI-powered ad targeting and automation scaled sales without requiring additional manual work.

$

Step 8: Integrate Fast Money Into Your Foundation

Fast money accelerates easy money growth. Properly allocated, it provides capital for scaling automated systems.

Step-by-Step Implementation:

1. Allocate a portion of fast-money gains to easy-money systems.

2. Use AI to optimize allocation and predict returns.

3. Maintain separate monitoring to ensure that fast-money volatility does not disrupt stable systems.

Example:

Jordan used profits from a short-term product flip to fund

an AI-managed digital service, creating a predictable revenue stream that compounded monthly.

$

Actionable Checklist for Building Your Easy Money Foundation

1. Automate savings, revenue, and expense tracking.

2. Choose predictable, low-effort income streams.

3. Reinvest profits for compounding growth.

4. Leverage time, technology, and outsourcing.

5. Continuously monitor and optimize systems.

6. Implement legal, financial, and operational safeguards.

7. Scale systems gradually while reinvesting intelligently.

8. Integrate fast-money gains to accelerate foundation growth.

9. Document all systems and processes for replicability.

$

Conclusion of Chapter 14

An easy-money foundation is **the bedrock of wealth**, ensuring long-term stability, compounding growth, and lifestyle freedom. By automating income streams, leveraging AI and outsourcing, reinvesting strategically, and monitoring systems carefully, anyone can build predictable, scalable, and resilient wealth.

When combined with fast money — the fuel of growth — this foundation allows readers to **maximize both opportunity and security**, creating a financial system that grows steadily, compounds reliably, and withstands the challenges of both personal and global economic changes.

The next chapter will present **the 50/30 Wealth Split Strategy**, a practical plan to integrate fast and easy money, ensuring both growth and stability.

Chapter 15
The 50/30 Wealth Split Strategy

By now, readers understand the importance of both **fast money and easy money**. Fast money fuels opportunity, while easy money provides a stable, compounding foundation. But knowing this is not enough — **you need a concrete plan** to allocate resources effectively and consistently.

This chapter introduces the **50/30 Wealth Split Strategy**, a practical formula to ensure that your earnings work efficiently, minimize risk, and maximize long-term growth. This system is actionable for anyone, whether in developed or emerging economies, and leverages **AI, automation, and disciplined allocation**.

$

The 50/30/20 Allocation Explained

The strategy divides your financial resources into three actionable buckets:

1. **50% → Long-Term Wealth (Foundation):**

    o Invest half of your fast-money profits into easy-money systems: automated digital businesses, rental income, dividend portfolios, and other compounding income streams.

    o Goal: Ensure stability and growth over years.

2. **30% → Reinvest Into Growth (Fuel):**

    o Allocate 30% to expanding fast-money ventures or testing new high-return opportunities.

    o Goal: Accelerate earnings and capitalize on new opportunities.

3. **20% → Lifestyle or Debt Elimination (Security & Freedom):**

    o Allocate the remaining 20% for living expenses, personal

enjoyment, or paying down high-interest debt.

o Goal: Maintain quality of life and reduce financial stress without jeopardizing investment growth.

Observation:

This strategy ensures that fast-money gains are **never spent recklessly** and that easy-money foundations grow consistently.

$

Step 1: Calculate Your Profit Pools

Before implementing the 50/30 Strategy, determine your total available profits from all fast-money ventures:

1. Identify net profit after expenses and taxes.

2. Calculate 50% for long-term wealth, 30% for reinvestment, and 20% for lifestyle or debt reduction.

3. Document each allocation in a ledger or AI-driven financial dashboard for accountability.

Example:

- Jordan and Leila earned $10,000 from a short-term product flip:

    o $5,000 → easy-money investments (digital products, rental units).

    o $3,000 → reinvested into new high-return ventures.

    o $2,000 → lifestyle upgrades and debt repayment.

$

Step 2: Build the Foundation with the 50% Bucket

Half of your profits should **secure long-term, stable income streams**:

1. **Digital Products:** AI tools can automate content creation, marketing, and sales funnels.

2. **Rental Income:** Use property management software to streamline operations.

3. **Investments:** Dividend-paying stocks, ETFs, and bonds managed with AI robo-advisors.

4. **Automated Online Businesses:** Subscription services, SaaS tools, or microservices platforms.

Practical Exercise:
Identify at least three easy-money channels to invest your 50% allocation. Use AI tools to simulate expected returns and growth rates over 1, 3, 5, and 10 years.

$

Step 3: Reinvest 30% Into Growth

The 30% bucket fuels **expansion and experimentation**:

1. **Scale Existing Ventures:** Use the capital to increase capacity, inventory, or reach.

2. **Test New Ventures:** Small, calculated experiments with measurable KPIs.

3. **Leverage AI:** Predict trends, optimize pricing, and manage marketing campaigns.

Example:
Jordan allocated $3,000 to test an online service marketplace. AI tools analyzed competitor pricing, optimized ads, and automated customer responses. Within two months, the venture generated $1,200 profit, feeding back into the system.

$

Step 4: Use 20% for Lifestyle and Debt Elimination

The final 20% ensures **financial security and quality of life**:

1. **Pay Down Debt:** Reduce interest burden to increase net profits in the future.

2. **Maintain Lifestyle:** Reward yourself without jeopardizing wealth-building goals.

3. **Emergency Fund:** Maintain liquidity to manage unexpected expenses or market fluctuations.

Practical Exercise:
Allocate your 20% proportionally across lifestyle needs, debt repayment, and emergency funds. Track spending to prevent overextension.

$

Step 5: Integrate AI for Precision Allocation

AI can make the 50/30 Wealth Split Strategy **more efficient and less error-prone:**

- Use AI-driven budgeting tools to automatically allocate funds into each bucket.

- Predict optimal reinvestment strategies for the 30% growth bucket.

- Monitor performance of long-term investments in real time to adjust allocations.

- Simulate market scenarios and potential gains to optimize decision-making.

Example:

Alex and Maya integrated AI dashboards to track all their investments and profits. The AI system suggested adjusting allocations between easy-money systems and new ventures, increasing long-term returns by 15% annually.

$

Step 6: Maintain Discipline and Accountability

Discipline is critical. The strategy works **only if followed consistently**:

1. Allocate funds immediately after profits are realized.

2. Avoid lifestyle creep that consumes more than the 20% bucket.

3. Reevaluate allocations quarterly to adjust for growth or unexpected gains/losses.

4. Document all decisions and outcomes to refine the system over time.

Emerging Economy Application:
Even with variable income, this disciplined allocation ensures consistent investment in long-term wealth, preventing volatility from undermining progress.

$

Step 7: Scale Over Time

Once the 50/30 system is operational, growth becomes **self-reinforcing**:

- Fast-money ventures feed easy-money systems.

- Easy-money foundations compound and increase available capital for reinvestment.

- AI assists in identifying new opportunities and adjusting allocations for optimal growth.

Example:
Jordan and Leila's initial $10,000 allocation to the 50/30 system compounded into $100,000 over 18 months due to reinvestment, scaling, and AI-assisted automation.

$

Step 8: Leverage Emerging Opportunities

The strategy is particularly effective in emerging economies:

1. **Digital Global Markets:** AI allows local entrepreneurs to compete globally.

2. **Micro-ventures:** Low capital fast-money projects fund automated easy-money systems.

3. **Technology Leverage:** AI tools compensate for limited local infrastructure.

Practical Implementation:

- Use mobile payment systems and AI to manage digital products.

- Reinvest fast-money micro-ventures into scalable digital platforms.

- Automate marketing and sales to reach global audiences without physical infrastructure.

$

Step 9: Monitor, Review, and Optimize

Consistency ensures the strategy works:

1. Track KPIs for each bucket (profit, ROI, compounding growth).

2. Use AI dashboards to simulate future scenarios and adjust allocations.

3. Adjust the 50/30/20 split based on performance, market conditions, and personal goals.

4. Document lessons learned to refine the system over time.

$

Case Study: Applying the 50/30 Wealth Split

Scenario:

- Jordan and Leila earned $20,000 in fast-money profits.

- o 50% ($10,000) → AI-managed digital courses generating $500/month passive income.

- o 30% ($6,000) → Tested two new e-commerce ventures, one generating $1,500 profit within two months.

- o 20% ($4,000) → Paid down personal debt and upgraded lifestyle moderately.

Outcome:

- Passive income streams now generate consistent cash flow.

- New ventures provide additional capital for future reinvestment.

- Lifestyle upgrades maintain quality of life without threatening financial stability.

The 50/30 system turned volatile gains into **predictable, scalable, and compounding wealth**.

$

Actionable Checklist for the 50/30 Wealth Split Strategy

1. Determine net profits from fast-money ventures.

2. Allocate 50% to long-term easy-money systems.

3. Allocate 30% to reinvestment in growth ventures.

4. Allocate 20% for lifestyle, debt, and emergencies.

5. Automate allocations using AI tools or financial software.

6. Track and document results quarterly.

7. Adjust allocations based on performance and opportunities.

8. Reinvest fast-money profits to strengthen easy-money foundations.

9. Scale AI systems to automate, predict, and optimize growth globally.

10. Maintain discipline and accountability to prevent deviation from the plan.

$

Conclusion of Chapter 15

The **50/30 Wealth Split Strategy** is the practical bridge between **fast money and easy money**. It provides a structured method to allocate resources, protect gains, and compound wealth consistently. By integrating automation, AI tools, and disciplined reinvestment, anyone can turn volatile profits into **sustainable, scalable, and resilient wealth**.

With this strategy, readers now have a **clear roadmap** for managing their earnings: balancing growth, stability, and lifestyle while preparing for long-term financial independence.

The next chapter will focus on **Chapter 16 —
Wealth for Life**, where we explore **generational systems, legacy planning, and strategies to ensure your wealth outlives you**.

Chapter 16
Wealth for Life (A Permanent Plan)

Wealth is most meaningful when it lasts. Building money that sustains a lifetime, supports a family, and creates opportunities for future generations requires a strategic approach far beyond fast flips or even steady passive income. It requires **planning, structure, legal protection, and disciplined execution**.

This chapter explores **how to create wealth that endures**, drawing lessons from both couples — Jordan and Leila, who experienced the highs and volatility of fast money, and Alex and Maya, who built a slow but compounding easy-money foundation. By the end, readers will understand **how to transform temporary gains into permanent wealth**, using modern tools including AI, digital platforms, and structured legacy systems.

$

The True Goal: Wealth That Outlives You

Temporary wealth can be exciting, but **it can vanish quickly** if mismanaged or if life circumstances change. Wealth for life is different — it is **resilient, generational, and systematized**.

Key characteristics of permanent wealth include:

1. **Predictability:** Income streams that continue even during economic turbulence.

2. **Scalability:** Systems that grow in value without constant manual labor.

3. **Protection:** Legal and financial safeguards against loss, mismanagement, or fraud.

4. **Legacy:** Structures to pass assets efficiently to heirs and future beneficiaries.

Observation:
Fast money provides opportunity, and easy money provides compounding growth — but neither guarantees permanence unless intentionally structured for longevity.

$

Step 1: Document Your Assets and Systems

Permanent wealth begins with **full transparency and clarity**. Without a detailed understanding of your assets, income streams, and obligations, it's impossible to plan for longevity.

Actionable Steps:

1. List all assets, including:

   o Cash, investments, properties, and digital assets.

   o Fast-money ventures, both active and inactive.

   o Easy-money systems: online businesses, dividends, and automated platforms.

2. Include liabilities:

   o Mortgages, business loans, credit cards, and pending obligations.

3. Use AI-driven financial dashboards to categorize assets, predict cash flow, and simulate growth scenarios over decades.

Example:

Alex and Maya used AI software to consolidate digital product revenue, rental income, and investment portfolios. The tool projected passive income growth for the next 10, 20, and 30 years, helping them plan reinvestments and legal structures.

$

Step 2: Build Legal Structures to Protect Wealth

Without proper legal structures, wealth — even significant fast or easy money gains — can be lost to lawsuits, poor estate planning, or taxes.

Key Legal Tools:

1. **Trusts:**

   o Protect assets from creditors, taxes, and mismanagement.

      o Control distribution to heirs over time rather than all at once.

2. **Corporations and LLCs:**

      o Separate personal and business assets to reduce liability.

      o Enhance tax efficiency and simplify succession planning.

3. **Wills and Estate Plans:**

      o Clearly define inheritance plans and contingencies.

      o Prevent disputes and delays during wealth transfer.

AI Tip:

- AI-driven legal platforms can generate trust and corporate documents efficiently.

- Predictive analytics can simulate tax scenarios to optimize estate plans.

Example:
Jordan set up a series of LLCs for fast-money ventures and a family trust for all long-term investments. This ensured that even if a high-risk venture failed, the core wealth was protected.

$

Step 3: Implement Automated Wealth Systems

Automation ensures **wealth continuity without constant oversight**. By integrating AI and digital tools, permanent wealth can **grow and manage itself**:

1. **Investment Automation:**

   o Robo-advisors allocate and rebalance portfolios.

   o Dividends and interest are reinvested automatically.

2. **Business Automation:**

   o AI handles digital product sales, customer support, and marketing campaigns.

- E-commerce operations can scale globally without local staff.

3. **Cash Flow Management:**

   - AI budgeting tools track profits, losses, and reinvestment allocations.

   - Alerts notify of underperforming streams or opportunities for optimization.

Emerging Economy Application:
Even with limited local infrastructure, entrepreneurs can use AI, digital banking, and mobile money to automate global revenue streams.

$

Step 4: Plan for Generational Wealth

Wealth is only permanent if it **survives beyond your lifetime**. Generational planning includes:

1. **Structured Distribution:**

   o Decide what assets go to children, family members, or charitable causes.

   o Use trusts to control timing and conditions of inheritance.

2. **Education and Training:**

   o Teach heirs financial literacy and wealth management principles.

   o Introduce them gradually to control over assets, avoiding mismanagement.

3. **Succession Planning:**

   o Appoint managers or guardians for complex business and investment structures.

   o Use AI dashboards to maintain oversight even remotely.

Example:

Maya set up a family trust where rental income was reinvested, digital business profits were partially distributed, and children received financial literacy training each year. This ensured wealth continuity and responsible management.

$

Step 5: Use Fast Money to Accelerate Permanent Wealth

Fast money gains can be **strategically channeled into long-term systems**:

1. Allocate a portion to your easy-money foundation using the **50/30 strategy**.

2. Use high-yield ventures to fund diversified investments, real estate, or digital platforms.

3. Avoid lifestyle inflation that undermines reinvestment.

Example:
Jordan took profits from a high-risk e-commerce venture and funded an automated online education platform. Within months, the platform created a stable, compounding revenue stream.

$

Step 6: Protect Wealth Against Risks

Even permanent wealth is vulnerable without protection. Consider:

1. **Insurance:** Property, business, health, and life insurance safeguard assets.

2. **Diversification:** Spread investments across industries, regions, and asset classes.

3. **Risk Monitoring:** AI tools can track market trends, detect anomalies, and forecast crises.

4. **Legal Safeguards:** Trusts, LLCs, and estate plans reduce exposure to claims and disputes.

Emerging Economy Application:
AI risk monitoring can provide insights into currency fluctuations, political instability, or market shocks, enabling timely strategic adjustments.

$

Step 7: Track, Review, and Adapt Systems

Wealth is dynamic; permanent systems must **adapt over time**.

1. Quarterly reviews: Use AI dashboards to track cash flow, investments, and business performance.

2. Scenario simulations: Predict outcomes of various market conditions.

3. Adjust reinvestment strategies: Shift fast-money profits to maintain balance and growth.

4. Maintain documentation: Record decisions and lessons to ensure continuity.

Example:
Alex and Maya review their digital businesses, rental portfolios, and investments quarterly using AI dashboards. This allows them to reallocate capital, upgrade automation, and maintain steady growth without increasing labor.

$

Step 8: Leave a Legacy Beyond Money

True wealth is not only about dollars — it is about **impact**:

1. Charitable giving and social investments.

2. Mentorship or education programs for family and community.

3. Documenting financial principles and systems for heirs.

Practical Exercise:

- Identify one charitable cause and one family education initiative to fund annually.

- Document operational principles and values behind each easy-money system for heirs.

$

Step 9: Integrate AI Across All Systems

AI is the **ultimate tool for wealth preservation and growth**:

- Portfolio optimization and risk prediction.

- Automated reporting and cash flow monitoring.

- Predictive analytics for emerging fast-money opportunities.

- AI assistants for operational management of businesses and rentals.

Emerging Economy Application:
With AI, entrepreneurs can globally scale automated systems, hedge against local economic instability, and

maintain generational wealth with minimal local infrastructure.

$

Step 10: Continuous Learning and Adaptation

Permanent wealth is built by **people who learn, adapt, and innovate**:

1. Keep up with financial education, emerging AI tools, and market trends.

2. Experiment cautiously with new fast-money or easy-money strategies.

3. Document successful frameworks to integrate into the permanent wealth system.

Example:
Jordan and Leila continuously test new AI-driven business models, reinvesting select profits into their easy-money foundation. Over a decade, these iterations compound into a self-sustaining wealth ecosystem.

$

Actionable Checklist for Wealth for Life

1. Document all assets, liabilities, and income streams.

2. Implement legal structures: trusts, LLCs, corporations, and estate plans.

3. Automate easy-money systems and integrate AI for monitoring and optimization.

4. Allocate fast-money profits strategically into long-term wealth streams.

5. Establish generational plans: education, succession, and structured distribution.

6. Protect assets through insurance, diversification, and legal safeguards.

7. Review and adapt systems quarterly with AI analytics.

8. Leave a legacy through philanthropy, mentorship, and documentation.

9. Continuously learn, innovate, and integrate new strategies and technologies.

$

Conclusion of Chapter 16

Wealth that lasts is **intentional, structured, and adaptive**. By combining the fast-money engine with a robust easy-money foundation, implementing disciplined allocation strategies, and leveraging AI and automation, anyone can build **wealth that endures a lifetime and extends to future generations**.

This chapter has provided a **step-by-step roadmap** for creating permanent wealth: legal structures, automation, AI tools, and generational strategies. Readers are now equipped not only to grow money but to **protect, multiply, and pass it on**, ensuring their financial legacy is secure, scalable, and resilient.

The next chapter will summarize the journey and provide **final strategies for balancing fast and easy money**, empowering readers to transform their financial lives permanently.

Chapter 17
Conclusion: Money That Changes Your Life

The journey through fast money and easy money is not just a financial education — it is a **transformation of mindset, strategy, and lifestyle**. By now, you have met two couples: Jordan and Leila, the Fast Money Couple, who chase opportunity with speed and courage, and Alex and Maya, the Easy Money Couple, who build wealth steadily through predictability, automation, and discipline.

In this conclusion, we synthesize the lessons, strategies, and practical applications from both worlds. We will also expand the discussion to **emerging economies**, where the combination of fast and easy money, powered by AI and technology, can unlock unprecedented financial freedom.

$

The Core Lessons from Both Couples

1. Fast Money Provides Fuel

- o Fast money is the engine that generates opportunity, capital, and momentum.

- o It thrives on speed, risk-taking, and action.

- o The psychological triggers — urgency, scarcity, and ambition — drive quick results.

- o **Key Lesson:** Fast money is powerful but fleeting unless directed into systems that preserve and grow wealth.

2. Easy Money Provides Foundation

- o Easy money is steady, compounding, and resilient.

- o It prioritizes predictability, discipline, and long-term thinking.

- o Systems, automation, and reinvestment make wealth grow in the background, like a tree slowly but consistently reaching for the sky.

- o **Key Lesson:** Easy money is not glamorous, but it protects mental health, relationships, and lifestyle while compounding financial growth.

3. **The Integration of Both Worlds**

- o Fast money and easy money are **complementary, not contradictory**.

- o Fast money accelerates growth; easy money stabilizes it.

- o The synergy ensures wealth is both **rapidly generated and permanently preserved**.

$

The Two-Bucket Wealth Model Revisited

The **Two-Bucket Wealth Model** is the strategic framework that balances both approaches:

1. **Fast Money Bucket (Fuel)**

   o Generate rapid capital through short-term ventures, high-risk plays, and side hustles.

   o Reinforce learning, agility, and market awareness.

2. **Easy Money Bucket (Foundation)**

   o Channel profits from fast money into automated, predictable, and scalable income streams.

   o Protect wealth, compound returns, and build a long-term foundation.

Implementation Tip:
The **50/30 Wealth Split Strategy** operationalizes this model. Allocate 50% to the foundation, 30% to reinvestment, and 20% to lifestyle and debt management.

Over time, the combination of buckets ensures both **growth and stability**.

$

Actionable Steps to Transform Fast Money Into Permanent Wealth

1. **Document Everything**

   o Track fast-money gains, easy-money systems, and reinvestment strategies.

   o AI dashboards are invaluable for monitoring cash flow, analyzing performance, and forecasting growth.

2. **Systematize Fast Money**

   o Standardize processes for sourcing, testing, and scaling fast-money ventures.

   o Use AI to automate data collection, trend prediction, and customer outreach.

3. **Reinvest Strategically**

   o Allocate a portion of profits to easy-money systems.

   o Diversify into digital products, rentals, dividend portfolios, and automated businesses.

4. **Protect Your Wealth**

   o Legal structures: LLCs, corporations, and trusts.

   o Insurance: Property, liability, and life.

   o Documentation: Contracts, agreements, and estate plans.

5. **Automate Easy Money Systems**

   o AI-driven marketing, sales, and customer management.

   o Robo-advisors for investments.

   o Automated rental or subscription management.

6. **Plan for Generational Wealth**

   o Structured distribution through trusts or legal entities.

   o Education for heirs in financial literacy and system management.

   o Documentation of principles, procedures, and values.

$

AI and Technology: Game Changers for Emerging Economies

Emerging economies face unique challenges: limited infrastructure, inconsistent banking systems, and unstable markets. Yet **AI and digital technology offer transformative opportunities**:

1. **Digital Fast Money Opportunities**

   o Freelancing, e-commerce, print-on-demand, and

microservices can scale globally.

o AI tools assist with automation, client management, content creation, and trend prediction.

2. **Easy Money Automation**

o Mobile wallets, digital banking, and automated investment platforms allow compounding wealth even in low-resource environments.

o AI manages risk, forecasts growth, and optimizes reinvestment strategies.

3. **Bridging Fast and Easy Money**

o Short-term profits from digital ventures fund automated income streams, creating resilience against local economic volatility.

Example:
A solo entrepreneur in Southeast Asia can launch a small

e-commerce business (fast money) and reinvest profits into an automated online course platform (easy money), leveraging AI to manage customer interactions, marketing, and analytics. Within months, they achieve **predictable, scalable, and globally competitive income**.

$$\$$$

Practical Scripts, Templates, and Checklists

Readers now have a blueprint for action:

1. **Fast Money Checklist**
   - Identify high-return, low-capital opportunities.
   - Test ideas quickly with small investments.
   - Document all processes.
   - Automate and outsource repetitive tasks.
   - Know exit strategies for each venture.

2. **Easy Money Checklist**

- o Automate savings and income streams.

- o Diversify digital products, rental income, and investments.

- o Reinvest systematically to compound wealth.

- o Integrate AI for monitoring, forecasting, and optimization.

3. **Integration Checklist**

- o Allocate profits using the 50/30 Wealth Split Strategy.

- o Maintain discipline in lifestyle and reinvestment.

- o Review systems quarterly with AI analytics.

- o Document lessons and refine processes continuously.

4. **Emerging Economy Additions**

   o Use mobile payment solutions for automation.

   o Leverage global digital platforms for fast-money ventures.

   o Reinvest profits in low-effort, scalable systems.

   o Monitor risks using AI tools tailored to local markets.

$

Behavioral and Psychological Insights

Wealth is as much about **mindset** as money. Lessons from both couples include:

- **Discipline:** Consistently allocate, reinvest, and protect wealth.

- **Patience:** Easy money systems take time but compound exponentially.

- **Adaptability:** Fast money requires flexibility, and AI can augment decision-making.

- **Accountability:** Track results and adjust systematically.

- **Vision:** Wealth for life is about generational impact, not just immediate gratification.

Key Takeaway:
Success is not luck — it is the **alignment of behavior, systems, and strategy**.

$

Balancing Lifestyle and Wealth

Both couples illustrate that financial transformation is also about **life transformation**:

- Fast money without boundaries creates stress, burnout, and relationship strain.

- Easy money without initiative can feel stagnant or slow.

- Combining the two allows:

  - Freedom to enjoy life without sacrificing growth.

  - Financial resilience against emergencies.

  - Ability to invest in personal development, family, and community.

$

Emerging Technologies for Wealth Multiplication

AI and related technologies are no longer optional — they are **essential tools for modern wealth-building**:

1. **Predictive Analytics** – Identify high-demand products, services, or investment opportunities before competitors.

2. **Automation** – AI automates customer service, marketing, inventory, and finance.

3. **Global Market Access** – Reach customers worldwide, bypassing local limitations.

4. **Risk Management** – Predict market fluctuations and optimize resource allocation.

Practical Tip:
Even small fast-money projects in emerging economies can generate compounding returns when paired with AI-driven easy-money systems.

$

Final Framework: Your Path to Financial Transformation

1. **Start Fast, Start Now:** Begin with a small fast-money project, test, and learn.

2. **Build Systems:** Automate both fast and easy money wherever possible.

3. **Allocate Wisely:** Use the 50/30 Wealth Split Strategy to balance growth, reinvestment, and lifestyle.

4. **Protect Everything:** Legal structures, diversification, and AI monitoring safeguard assets.

5. **Compound Wealth:** Reinvest fast-money profits into easy-money systems to create long-term stability.

6. **Plan for Generations:** Document, educate, and establish trusts to secure wealth beyond your lifetime.

7. **Leverage AI:** Continuously use AI tools to optimize, predict, and scale.

8. **Adapt and Iterate:** Treat wealth as a living system — monitor, learn, and refine continuously.

$$\$$

Key Takeaways from Jordan and Leila (Fast Money)

- **Action and speed matter.** Opportunities lost today may never return.

- **Emotion can be both a motivator and a risk.** Discipline converts adrenaline into profit.

- **Reinvestment is critical.** Fast gains without strategy evaporate quickly.

$

Key Takeaways from Alex and Maya (Easy Money)

- **Patience pays.** Compounding and automation create long-term stability.

- **Predictability protects relationships and lifestyle.** Stress is minimized.

- **Scalability ensures generational wealth.** Systems outlive their creators when properly structured.

$

Your Next Steps

1. **Assess your current finances** – Identify fast-money potential and easy-money opportunities.

2. **Document and systematize** – Use AI dashboards for clarity and monitoring.

3. **Apply the 50/30 Strategy** – Allocate resources intentionally.

4. **Protect your foundation** – Legal structures, insurance, and diversification are mandatory.

5. **Build generational systems** – Trusts, estate plans, and education ensure longevity.

6. **Leverage AI for growth** – Predict trends, automate processes, and scale globally.

$

Conclusion

The money that changes your life is **not just dollars — it is strategy, systems, and discipline combined with vision.** By integrating fast money with easy money, implementing automated and AI-enhanced systems, and planning for both the present and the future, you can achieve **financial freedom, lifestyle balance, and generational wealth.**

Emerging economies present unique challenges, but they also provide **opportunity for exponential growth** when digital technology and AI are leveraged effectively. Fast money gives you the speed; easy money gives you the stability; together, they create a **wealth ecosystem that is resilient, scalable, and permanent.**

Your financial transformation begins today. **Take action, systematize, and commit to growth**, and the money you earn will not only change your life — it will change your legacy.

APPENDICES
A-E

Appendix A
CHECKLISTS FOR WEALTH MANAGEMENT

This appendix contains step-by-step checklists to ensure readers implement both fast and easy money systems effectively.

1. Fast Money Checklist

- Identify high-return, low-capital opportunities.

- Test ideas with minimal risk.

- Document processes and results.

- Automate repetitive tasks using AI tools.

- Know exit strategies for every venture.

- Allocate profits according to 50/30/20 strategy.

2. Easy Money Checklist

- Automate savings, investments, and income streams.

- Set up digital products, rental income, or dividend portfolios.

- Reinvest consistently to compound wealth.

- Use AI dashboards to track performance and growth.

- Monitor and optimize systems quarterly.

- Document lessons and refine systems for longevity.

3. Integration Checklist

- Allocate fast-money profits to easy-money systems systematically.

- Reinvest 30% of profits into growth ventures.

- Keep lifestyle spending within 20% of profits.

- Review allocations quarterly with AI analytics.

- Protect assets legally and financially.

- Plan for generational transfer of wealth.

Appendix B
FAST MONEY CALCULATORS

These calculators help readers evaluate fast-money opportunities, potential returns, and risks.

1. Fast Money ROI Calculator

- Input: Initial investment, expected revenue, expected expenses.

- Output: Net profit, ROI %, and payback period.

2. Risk Assessment Calculator

- Input: Probability of success, potential loss, and potential gain.

- Output: Weighted expected value to guide decision-making.

3. Time-to-Profit Calculator

- Input: Hours invested, expected profit.

- Output: Profit per hour to compare multiple opportunities.

AI INTEGRATION TIP:
Use AI tools to simulate multiple fast-money scenarios simultaneously, adjusting variables to optimize returns.

Appendix C
EASY MONEY INVESTMENT
STARTER PACK

This appendix provides a starter framework for easy-money systems, including platforms, tools, and recommended approaches.

1. Digital Products

- Platforms: Teachable, Gumroad, Udemy.

- Tools: Canva, ChatGPT, Grammarly for content creation.

- Automation: Email sequences, chatbots, and subscription billing.

2. Passive Income Investments

- Dividend ETFs, REITs, and high-yield bonds.

- Robo-advisors for automatic portfolio management.

- Reinvestment strategy to compound growth over time.

3. Rental Income

- Platforms: Airbnb, Vrbo, local property management systems.

- Automation: Booking management, AI chatbots, and dynamic pricing tools.

4. Automated Business Ventures

- Print-on-demand, SaaS platforms, or subscription services.

- Use AI for marketing, analytics, and customer support.

EXTRA TIP:
Start with one system in each category, automate as much as possible, and scale gradually.

Appendix D
30-DAY ACTION PLAN

This plan guides readers to take immediate action toward building fast and easy money systems.

Week 1 — Assessment & Planning

- Document current financial status, assets, and liabilities.

- Identify fast-money opportunities with minimal risk.

- Identify easy-money income systems to implement.

Week 2 — System Setup

- Automate savings and investments for easy money.

- Launch first fast-money project.

- Set up dashboards and tracking systems using AI tools.

Week 3 — Implementation

- Reinvest first profits into easy-money systems.

- Optimize processes using AI analytics.

- Begin documentation of processes for replication and future scaling.

Week 4 — Review & Scale

- Evaluate first results for both fast and easy money.

- Adjust allocations according to the 50/30/20 strategy.

- Identify one new fast-money opportunity and one new easy-money system for the next 30 days.

EXTRA TIP:
Repeat this cycle monthly, gradually increasing automation, reinvestment, and wealth compounding.

Appendix E
SOURCES CITED

This appendix lists references, tools, and studies used throughout the book to ensure credibility and allow further research.

Sources Include:

- Financial studies on risk-taking and compounding wealth.

- Research on behavioral psychology in money management.

- Guides and resources for digital product creation, passive income, and investment platforms.

- AI tool manuals and predictive analytics reports.

- Legal guides on trusts, LLCs, estate planning, and asset protection.

EXTRA TIP:
Always verify local regulations and market conditions when implementing strategies, especially in emerging economies.

FAST MONEY EASY MONEY

PROVEN SYSTEMS THAT ARE TIME TESTED AND WILL WORK IN EMERGING ECONOMIES UTILIZING AI TECH

THE ART & ARTIST

Want to make money fast *and* build lasting wealth by also leveraging AI and other technologies? ***FAST MONEY, EASY MONEY: Unlock the Secrets of Wealth with a Proven, Step-by-Step System*** (the third work by Braxton R. Meeks) is your ultimate blueprint.

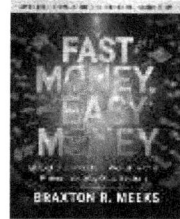

This revolutionary guide reveals the secrets of two couples — one mastering high-speed, high-risk income, the other creating automated, steady, passive wealth — and shows how to combine their strategies for maximum financial success.

Inside, you'll discover:

- **Fast money tactics** to generate immediate cash flow from side hustles, flipping, and AI-powered ventures.
- **Easy money systems** that create predictable, automated income streams, from digital products to dividends and rentals.

- **The Two-Bucket Wealth Model** to protect long-term wealth while fueling growth.
- **50/30/20 Profit Allocation Strategy** to reinvest, save, and enjoy life without risk.
- **Step-by-step templates, checklists, and calculators** to take immediate action.

Perfect for beginners, aspiring entrepreneurs, or anyone ready to **transform their financial future**, Braxton R. Meeks' *FAST MONEY, EASY MONEY* released in January 2026 by BePublished.org teaches you how to move fast, grow steadily, and create wealth that lasts generations. Take control today — fast, safe, and permanent wealth is within your reach!

FAST MONEY, EASY MONEY reveals the exact strategies, mindsets, and systems used by two couples who mastered wealth in radically different ways — then shows you how to combine their methods into a single, powerful financial roadmap.

Whether you're just starting out or want to maximize your current income, this book provides a complete blueprint to create financial freedom, protect your wealth, and build a life that lasts — not just for you, but for generations to come.

Take control of your financial destiny. Learn from the "Fast Money Couple" and the "Easy Money Couple," and implement strategies that work — today. Your wealth transformation starts here. Fast, safe, and permanent.

Available globally as a Kindle eBook, ***FAST MONEY, EASY MONEY: Unlock the Secrets of Wealth with a Proven, Step-by-Step System*** by Braxton R. Meeks may also be purchased for print as a softcover / paperback book from online and bricks-and-mortar book resellers including your favorite bookstore.

THE AUTHOR

Braxton R. Meeks of Central Mississippi is a truth-teller with a mission: to dismantle excuses, confront generational cycles of harm, and call families to higher standards of accountability and love. A proud product of homeschooling, he has been awarded an

honorary bachelor's degree along with an honorary master's degree in 2025 by Able University.

Making his literary debut with a double release in September 2025, Meeks presents two uncompromising works:

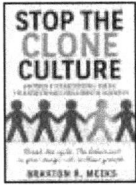

✓ **STOP THE CLONE CULTURE: Honest Parenting T hat Transforms Children & Society**

✓ **BLOOD TAUGHT ME: Healing From the Past, When Family Hurt**

Together, these books challenge readers to face uncomfortable realities — about how families shape us, how excuses weaken us, and how healing requires honesty, accountability, and courage.

Meeks writes with the conviction that every child deserves more than survival; they deserve the space, protection, and truth to become more than a copy of fractured adults. His work speaks to parents, adult children, and anyone ready to break cycles and build a healthier, more compassionate future.

In January 2026, he released this third work and first business-centered self-help book titled **FAST CASH, EASY CASH: Unlock the Secrets of Wealth with a Proven, Step-by-Step System**, Perfect for beginners, aspiring entrepreneurs, or anyone ready to transform their financial future, this book teaches you how to move fast, grow steadily, and create wealth that lasts generations.

When he isn't writing, Braxton Rhymes Meeks is usually at his cousin's barn engaged in community dialogue, mentoring, and equestrian engagements that bridge personal growth with social responsibility. His debut books are only the beginning of a larger body of work designed to spark transformation in families and society.